ENDING ABORTION

Not just fighting it!

Fr. Frank A. Pavone, M.E.V.

CATHOLIC BOOK PUBLISHING CORP.
New Jersey

Dedicated to the memory of

Pope John Paul II *for whom I served at the Pontifical Council for the Family and with whom I had the honor to discuss the cause of life;*

Blessed Mother Teresa of Calcutta *who personally encouraged the growth of Priests for Life and with whom I spent many hours talking about pro-life strategy;*

Cardinal John O'Connor *who ordained me to the priesthood, permitted me to lead Priests for Life, and taught me how to be a pro-life leader.*

They inspired me; they inspired the whole world; and their work lives on in the committed action of pro-life people today.

NIHIL OBSTAT: Fr. John Leies, S.M., S.T.D.
Censor Librorum

IMPRIMATUR: ✠ Most Rev. John W. Yanta
Bishop of Amarillo

Copyright © 2006 by Father Frank A. Pavone

ISBN 978-0-89942-138-4 (h/c)

ISBN 978-0-89942-131-5 (p/b)

Library of Congress Catalog Card Number: 2006930091

Grateful acknowledgment is made to the publications in which these essays first appeared.

Printed in the United States of America

1 2 3 4 5 6 7 8 9

Contents

Introduction

THIS book is for all people who oppose abortion and who want to end it.

Many people are pro-life privately, that is, in regard to their own participation in abortion. They would never do it, encourage it, or facilitate it. Most of us also have that attitude regarding violent crime and child abuse. Yet few if any would say that it suffices to "personally oppose" these acts. It is not enough to refrain from doing such things; we must create a society in which nobody feels free to do them.

Yet we treat the victims of abortion differently than the victims of crime or child abuse. The latter have protection despite the fact that some devalue them; the former are deprived of protection because some devalue them. And while it is clear that in a sinful world, sins will always be committed, we never have permission to tolerate sin or injustice. We work to bring them to an end.

That is why, in this book and in my pro-life activism since 1976, I have not tired of calling pro-life people to renew each day their goal to not simply reduce abortion or bear witness against abortion, but rather to end abortion. "Woe to you if you do not succeed in defending life," the Holy Father declared at World Youth Day in Denver in 1993. Woe to us, indeed. This war over abortion does not end in "Pro-life wins or Pro-choice wins." If pro-life doesn't win, nobody wins.

Abortion destroys everything it touches. For a government to permit abortion is to permit the disintegration of the state itself. No longer is such a nation the common home for all its people, but rather a tyrant state that disguises oppression in the language of rights. For a Church to permit abortion is to betray the Gospel and to render itself incapable of leading people to the healing forgiveness of

5

Christ. For an individual to permit abortion, turning the other way and failing to do his or her part to correct this injustice, is to betray the very meaning of being human: to be a person for others, aware that God has entrusted us to each other, and that we find our fulfillment only when we give ourselves away for the good of the other person.

The pages that follow contain my reflections on abortion and the pro-life movement from various angles. I have presented some of the key concepts to help readers focus on the fact that abortion is about people before it is about "issues." The person of the baby, the person of the mom and dad, the person who performs the procedure, the person who witnesses all of this as a bystander, the person who tries to stop this injustice—these are the subjects of my reflections. Abortion affects us all, compels a response from us all, and ultimately provides a measuring line by which God will judge us all.

The seriousness of my reflections on this tragedy are combined with the immense joy that comes from acknowledging that we are celebrating the victory of life. Jesus Christ is risen from the dead, and the entire Kingdom of death has been robbed of its power! Every bit of our pro-life activity, therefore, needs to be immersed in the awareness of this victory. Indeed, we are not just working for victory, we are working from victory!

It is my fervent prayer that these reflections will give readers the tools they need to reaffirm their own commitment to the pro-life cause as the pivotal human rights cause of our day, to articulate pro-life arguments convincingly and compassionately, and to carry out their role in the pro-life movement with the peace and joy that come only from God and that nobody can take away from them.

Part I
The Activists

The Warrior Soul

GENERAL George S. Patton, Jr., in his 1926 essay, "The Secret of Victory," wrote, "The secret of victory lies not wholly in knowledge. It lurks invisible in that vitalizing spark, intangible, yet as evident as the lightning—the warrior soul. The fixed determination to acquire the warrior soul, and having acquired it to either conquer or perish with honor, is the *secret of victory*."

I cannot count how many "warrior souls" I've met across the country in the pro-life movement. I think of the elderly woman who could not walk, yet confined to a wheelchair and battling with cancer, insisted on going regularly to the abortion mill to join the people praying on the sidewalk to save children about to be killed.

I think of the young people who relocate to unfamiliar parts of the country and, for little or no salary, undertake full-time pro-life work that brings them ridicule even from those they thought were their friends. Yet nothing matters more to them than stopping the killing.

I think of the pastor who told his people that if they didn't like his preaching on abortion, they could go elsewhere, but that he would be working to help all his brother priests to preach this message, so that there would be no parish where it wasn't heard.

I think of men and women I know in the media who challenge their colleagues to present the truth about abortion, and don't care that their colleagues ridicule them or that in some cases they may lose opportunities to advance in the company ladder. What matters most to them is the victory of the truth.

The litany can go on and on.

If we glimpse the depth of the horrific problem of abortion, and how entrenched it is in our society, there are two ways we might respond.

First, we can pretend that there is nothing that can be done, and end up either not engaged in the battle, or engaged in it as "a hobby," as something to be squeezed in when "more important" things aren't demanding our attention. And we never take on tasks that will either require too much sacrifice or prove wrong the idea that we cannot succeed.

The other response is to become the "warrior soul." While this is not "fanaticism," it is *total dedication*, to the point of being willing to give one's life in the cause. "Fanaticism" means that, except for the one focus we have, our personality shuts down and we disconnect from reality. The "warrior soul," on the other hand, devotes all of his fully functioning personality to his cause, and it is precisely because he *is connected* to reality that he sees that cause as all-important.

Social change doesn't come through committees and boards. It comes through warrior souls. It's something like what Scripture tells us: "The way we came to know love was that he laid down his life for us; so we ought to lay down our lives for our brothers" (1 Jn 3:16).

Three Simple Activities

WHAT simple pro-life activities can almost everyone do with very little effort, which bring the pro-life message to a large number of people who are not going to go out of their way to hear it, and which cost next to nothing?

Answer: the precious feet pin, pro-life bank checks, and pro-life bumper stickers.

1. **The Precious Feet.** Some 88% of abortions in the United States occur in the first twelve weeks of pregnancy. Most people still have no idea how well developed the preborn child is at the time when these abortions occur.

The Precious Feet pin shows the exact size and shape of a preborn child's feet at ten weeks after conception. It is an attractive and instructive pin, showing people, in a single glance, that the victim of abortion is one of us. The pin provides an excellent discussion-starter. Children also love to wear it, and in this way can bring the pro-life message to their own parents.

2. **Pro-life Bank Checks.** These checks carry an attractive pro-life picture or message, which varies from check to check within the same set. For example, some of them show a mother and child, others show the precious feet described above. Sayings include "Abortion stops a beating heart" and "Every Baby is Wanted by Someone."

Each time we write a check, about 15 people see it by the time it is returned to us. By using pro-life checks, we are therefore making numerous people aware of the message, without any extra time or trouble for ourselves.

The check company will place on your checks all the pertinent information you indicate, and will handle the process completely without any interruption in your service. Contact Priests for Life for more information.

3. **Bumperstickers.** People read bumperstickers. While they will make your car look less attractive, the lives that can be saved as a result will be a benefit that far outweighs the importance of the car's appearance.

Pro-life bumperstickers come in a wide variety of messages, colors, and sizes. Some of the messages include, "Love them Both" (showing a mother and her baby), "We Can Live Without Abortion," and "If It's Not a Baby, You're Not Pregnant!" Some bumperstickers also contain the phone numbers of local or national hotlines either for alternatives to abortion, or post-abortion counseling.

Hearts have been changed and lives have been saved by means of each of these simple activities. None of them cost very much, and once you start to use them, they each have an "automatic" quality to them: they keep speaking to people while your mind is on other things! They speak to them in a quiet and non-threatening way, and the people they speak to include those who do not want to hear the message! Yet unless the tragedy is faced, it cannot be ended! Help to break the silence about abortion by using these three simple activities, and by encouraging others to use them as well.

Mixed Signals

IF we want to change the way people think, talk, and act toward *unwanted* unborn children, we will need to change the way they think, talk, and act about *wanted* unborn children. Our approach to them either conveys the presence of a person or, well, of something less than a person. Take four simple examples.

First, even the best pro-life people will be heard saying, "I'm expecting a child." But if you are "expecting" someone, that person hasn't arrived yet. Our message is that the unborn child is *already* here, and is fully a person. A pregnant woman is already a mother who has a child. "I'm carrying a child" is more appropriate, and in counting how many children she has, the child she carries counts as one, not as a "half" or one "on the way."

This leads to the issue of *naming the child*. A pregnant mother is often asked if she has "picked out a name yet." In the Culture of Life, every person has a name. Delaying the practice of naming until birth only reinforces the idea that we don't have a person there until birth. *A name should be chosen and used as soon as one discovers she is pregnant.* The practical problem, of course, is not knowing the child's gender right away. I recommend, then, choosing two names. But the key is the timing of the decision. In other words, the names are *definitively* chosen by the time pregnancy is discovered. They are not just possible names. As soon as the gender is known, one of the two will stick.

Another very common practice reinforces the notion that a person exists only at birth. Notice how we celebrate *birthdays*, but do not celebrate *Firstdays*. Actually, the

Culture of Life should be distinguished by its custom of celebrating *the day the person began to exist*, which, of course, is nine months prior to one's birthday. True, we do not know the day with exact certitude, but that should not mean we ignore it altogether. We all existed, lived, and grew prior to our birthdays, and the celebration of a "Firstday" nine months before our birthday would send a meaningful message to our culture.

Finally, the sad reality of miscarriage is common. The Culture of Life recognizes that miscarriage is the loss of a child who is a whole person. It is not the loss of a *concept* or of a *possibility*, but of an actual child, who has a body. Where possible, of course, baptism is administered, even if conditionally, in case the child may still be alive. Every reasonable effort should be made, furthermore, to take the bodily remains of this child and commit them to the earth by a proper burial. Here we need the generous collaboration of cemeteries and churches so that this practice becomes more common.

Babies in the womb are real, full persons. These four steps would be good ways to continue to waken our culture to that simple fact.

Marching for Life

IN 1973, seven out of nine justices declared that the children in the womb are not persons under the Constitution. They thereby excluded a whole segment of the human family from the protection of the law, and from the recognition that all are created equal.

On every single day of the more than 30 years that have since passed, the older brothers and sisters of these children throughout America have called on the nation to restore love and protection to them. And each year tens of thousands of pro-lifers come to Washington, DC on the day of that tragic decision.

The March for Life on January 22 is a great annual family reunion for the pro-life movement. From across America they arrive by bus and plane, and gather for a midday rally on the Ellipse, between the White House and the Washington Monument. They are encouraged by speeches from pro-life leaders, legislators, and clergy. Miss Nellie Gray, who has led the March from the beginning, effectively calls the participants to focus on the goal of the pro-life movement: full protection of each and every human person from fertilization!

After the rally, the march itself takes the crowd on a route from the Ellipse to the Supreme Court, where prayers and hymns continue, and friends greet each other. Many also go to lobby their elected officials at this time. The whole event is well organized and peaceful.

Although most participants come only for the march itself, there is a full day of seminars on the previous day. Participants are educated in the life principles and taught practical strategies for defending life. This convention is open to all. The entire event concludes with a beautiful banquet, the Rose Dinner, which honors the many people who work in the pro-life movement.

What does the March actually accomplish?

1. *It gives voice to the children.* Yes, abortion continues unabated. But it does not continue unchallenged. The presence of marchers in Washington is a prophetic call to the government and to the nation. When a tragedy goes on and on, the voice of those who defend the victims must only increase, not fall silent.

2. *It gives encouragement to our friends in government.* Those in Congress who support the right to life need to hear from us. They need to see that we are out there in great numbers, so that they can continue to call for an end to abortion.

3. *It encourages us.* Participants come away from the March invigorated and inspired for another year of work. They see those laboring with them across the country, and know they are part of a great movement.

4. *It trains young leaders.* I received my own inspiration to be active in this movement when I attended the March for Life as a high school student. Countless other young people receive similar inspiration from this event each year.

For information on the March for Life program, plus hotel and travel arrangements, contact *March for Life, PO Box 90300, Washington, DC 20090, or call 202-543-3377; Email:* info@marchforlife.org; *website:* www.marchforlife.org.

Monuments to the Unborn:
A Threefold Significance

IN my pro-life travels throughout the United States, one of the recurring privileges I have had is to bless memorials to the pre-born children who are in danger of abortion or who have been aborted. Most of these memorials, of all sizes and shapes, have been made possible by the generosity of local councils of the Knights of Columbus. Supreme Knight Virgil Dechant reported in 2003 that the number of such memorials was 2,200.

These memorial stones, which began at a suggestion of Cardinal O'Connor, have a threefold significance.

First of all, a memorial stone is set up in memory of a person. The stones give witness to the forgotten person, the "stranger in the womb," as Pope John Paul II called the unborn child in his homily at Giants Stadium on October 5, 1995. The *Roe vs. Wade* decision states that "the word 'person,' as used in the Fourteenth Amendment, does not include the unborn" (*Roe vs. Wade,* at 158). The memorial stones cry out that the unborn *are indeed* persons. *Things* can get thrown away and forgotten; the dignity of persons, however, requires that they be remembered, especially if others have thrown them away.

A second significance of the stones is that they provide a place to grieve, particularly for the mothers and fathers of aborted children. One of the most difficult aspects of post-abortion grief is that there is no body to hold or to see. The grief the parent feels is, furthermore, not generally acknowledged as legitimate. After all, this mother has been told that abortion is her right and choice. As such mothers and fathers become more and more aware of how wrong that mentality is, however, they need an outlet for their grief, and they need something physical on which to focus that grief. The memorial stones tell them that their grief is legitimate, and that others share their sorrow.

Finally, as a third significance, the stones symbolize us, who bear witness to the sanctity of life. Scripture tells us we are "living stones." We are to do with our words and our actions what the stones do silently. We are to speak up for those who cannot speak for themselves, and to do it with a determination which, like the stone, is unshakable.

Next time you have a free afternoon, seek out the memorial stone to the unborn which is nearest to you. Spend some time looking at it, praying, and pondering its threefold message.

The Lord Himself, when some complained about the testimony which the disciples bore to Him, said that if they were silent, the very stones would cry out. Some in our society complain about the proclamation of the pro-life message. Some are silent when they should speak up. But the Lord's words are being fulfilled; the stones are crying out.

Attention, Clinic Workers!

A SIGNIFICANT chapter in the abortion war focuses on the people who staff abortion facilities, and how they can be in legal trouble for participating in, or not exposing, illegal activities. Being aware of how much illegal activity occurs in abortion clinics, and what the red flags are which indicate it may be happening, can enable employees to protect themselves, and can enable pro-life people to help those employees leave the clinics, eventually shutting them down.

What kind of illegal activities are we speaking about?

The list includes income tax evasion, Medicaid fraud, insurance fraud, money laundering, sexual harassment of employees, sexual assault of patients, physical assault of patients, statutory rape, health and safety issues within the clinic, and consumer fraud, among others.

These activities are rampant in abortion clinics, because these clinics are the most unregulated surgical facilities in the nation. After all, you can't practice vice virtuously, and when your conscience is so diluted that you can kill innocent babies, these other violations are small potatoes in comparison.

Now many people may think that the staff workers in these facilities—such as the receptionists, the assistants, the "counselors,"—are hard-core, fully-committed pro-abortion persons. But that is not the case. Many of them are against abortion, or don't even think about the moral aspects of it. And it does not take much to convince many of them to leave, especially if they realize they might be unwitting accomplices in illegal activity.

By letting these clinic workers know the kinds of illegal activities in which they may be implicated, we in the pro-life community can bring many of them out of the industry, and bring legal action against the clinics.

The website, www.clinicworker.com, which gives more details about how to detect this illegal activity, was established by my friend Mark Crutcher and his team at Life Dynamics, Inc. Regarding signs of possible income tax evasion, for example, one should ask questions like, Does your employer or director use multiple accounting ledgers?; Are financial records ever written in pencil?; Does the clinic ever fail to give receipts for cash payments?

In many of the areas mentioned above, one has a moral and even legal obligation to report actual or possible abuses. Moreover, if an employee knows of such situations, others do as well. The first person to bring forward such information is often protected if authorities can be led to apprehend those responsible, and rewards sometimes accompany the revelation of these crimes.

Pro-life people have an opportunity to alert clinic workers to this situation by means of a new poster and business cards available by calling (940) 380-8800, or through the website, www.clinicworker.com. The poster should be used at demonstrations at abortion sites, and it is particularly important to go there on days when *abortions are not being performed,* because staff persons present on those days are more likely to both notice and talk about these matters.

Let's use this new and powerful approach today!

The Unwilling Audience

IF you read carefully the Acts of the Apostles, you see a basic principle at work: we must bring the message to those unwilling to hear it. Paul and the other apostles did not wait to be invited to proclaim the Gospel. Their "permission" to preach it came from the command of our Lord, and their audience was pre-determined: *all the nations*. Naturally, preaching the Gospel is most pleasant when the hearers are willing, eager, and have already knocked on our door asking for the good news. But if we preach only to those who ask us to, we fail to reach multitudes who need to hear the message, and may not even realize that they have this need. The message itself tells us of our deepest needs.

Don't get me wrong—I am not one who belittles "preaching to the choir." The "choir" needs preaching, too. After all, if the choir does not do the singing, who will? Preaching to the choir is a particular form of preaching, consisting of nurturing the commitment of those already committed, deepening the conversion of those already converted, and guiding the activity of those already active.

But we must reach the far greater audience who will never come looking for the message we have.

This is especially urgent in regard to the sanctity of life, because in this arena, not only does a *message* have to be believed, but *lives* have to be saved. Not only do *viewpoints* have to be changed, but *victims* have to be protected. Perhaps the most important principle, then, for the pro-life movement to adopt at this point in time, is that *pro-life activity which relies on the voluntary consent of the audience is insufficient*. This is not to say that such activity is *unnecessary*, nor is this to say that such activity is *without value*.

It is, however, to say that the amount of time and energy our movement spends on such activity is out of all proportion to the amount of time and energy that is spent on reaching the unwilling audience.

To put it rather bluntly, effective social reform requires *forcing the message on an unwilling audience*. It means confronting the culture with what it does not want to hear. For example, along with preaching the pro-life message inside the church, where people freely go, we need to proclaim the pro-life message on the public sidewalk *outside* the church, where people can hear it whether they want to or not. This can take the form of prayerful life chains with effective posters, or literature distribution, or even special parades and motorcades.

The Supreme Court has repeatedly made it clear that what is protected by the First Amendment is precisely our freedom to speak a message to an audience that is opposed to it and even offended by it. It is part of the greatness of America that the unpopular message need not retreat only to the secret places where those who want it know how to find it.

A Sober Look at CPCs

FEW things are more inspiring in the pro-life movement than the generous and even heroic work of those
who serve the approximately 3,000 Pregnancy Resource
Centers around the country. There are more such centers
than there are abortion mills, and the bulk of the pro-life
movement, though you would never know this from the
media, consists of people providing financial, medical,
legal, religious, and emotional support to help mothers
avoid the temptation to abort.

But there also is the challenge. Are these centers actually reaching women who are tempted to abort? Many
report otherwise. For example, a center that said they
"saw 1,450 women in a year" also indicated that only 450
of these women took a pregnancy test. Of those, only 150
were actually pregnant, and of those, only 15 were considering abortion. It is certainly an integral aspect of
Christian service to assist pregnant mothers who would
never think about having an abortion. But the pro-life
movement has to be sure that its more specific mission of
stopping abortion is being fulfilled. We have to attract more
abortion-minded women to our centers.

A major step being taken in this direction is the effort
to convert pregnancy assistance centers to the status of
medical clinics. The advantage of this is that such clinics
would be under the supervision of a doctor and would be
able to administer a pregnancy test, use an ultrasound
machine, test for STDs, and give diagnoses. Currently
20% of CPCs have upgraded to medical clinics and another 100 are in the process of converting. "Pregnancy help
centers that have converted to medical clinics report a 40-
90% increase in the number of abortion-minded and abor-

tion-vulnerable clientele and an increase in the number of women who choose life" (www.nifla.org).

What, then, is needed to help this effort?

1. Become informed. Consult the National Institute of Family & Life Advocates (NIFLA) (www.nifla.org), which assists pregnancy centers to become medical clinics.

2. Pro-life physicians wanted! If you are, or know of, a physician who would be willing to volunteer some of his or her time to supervise such a medical clinic, let us know! "Supervising" does not require that the doctor actually be present at the clinic.

3. Talk up the idea! Many people can assist with legal help, adjustments in the physical facility that may be needed, ultrasound technology, and marketing.

4. Legislation is being introduced in Congress to fund such medical clinics so they can obtain the best ultrasound equipment. Inform yourself and support such legislation!

NIFLA hopes to assist 1,000 pregnancy centers to convert to medical clinics by the year 2010. There is no time to waste. Lives depend on it!

Finally, there is perhaps a lesson here for all who do pro-life work. We should never become self-satisfied, and should always seek to bring the best professional practices to our movement. Defenders of child-killing have done it for decades, and we have a cause far more just!

Conscientious Objection

POPE John Paul II wrote the following in *The Gospel of Life:*

"Abortion and euthanasia are thus crimes which no human law can claim to legitimize. There is no obligation in conscience to obey such laws; instead there is a *grave and clear obligation to oppose them by conscientious objection*" (EV, n. 73).

But what is this "conscientious objection?"

Certainly, conscience clauses protect doctors and nurses who refuse to perform or assist in abortions. There is also a clear obligation on the part of lawmakers to protect human life.

But an important arena for conscientious objection also lies in the non-medical service personnel who may be called upon to help an abortion facility. Some 90% of abortions are performed *outside* of hospitals. Like any facility, these abortion mills require servicing from a wide range of people. When the roof leaks, someone is called to fix it. When the heat or air conditioning fails, someone is called to service it. When the copy machine is broken, someone is called to repair it.

Is it not time for the People of Life to say that they will not cooperate in servicing abortion facilities? The fact that abortion is legal does not imply that any citizen, particularly one opposed in conscience to abortion, has to do anything to help it to happen. Putting aside the nuances about the forms of cooperation and the levels of obligation associated with them, is it not time for a *strong and pure witness* of *non-cooperation*?

Businesses need not contract with abortion facilities, and employees can refuse to take an assignment that brings them to an abortion mill. Many, in fact, may be servicing facilities without realizing that abortions are committed there. Local pro-life activists can find out which businesses service the local abortion facilities, and then begin informing the businesses and their employees of that fact.

Federal law, under Title VII, states, "It shall be an unlawful employment practice for an employer to fail or refuse to hire or to discharge any individual, or otherwise to discriminate against any individual with respect to his compensation, terms, conditions, or privileges of employment, because of such individual's . . . religion," and further indicates that "[t]he term 'religion' includes all aspects of religious observance and practice, as well as belief . . ." There is certainly a strong defense here for those who are opposed to abortion to refuse to service abortion facilities.

Let this witness begin, from plumbers, electricians, office supply companies, delivery services, printing companies, lawn and garden companies, snow removal services, computer consultants, office machine repair services, sanitation workers, roofing companies, taxi drivers, security companies, lock and key companies, cleaning and maintenance services, sign and fence companies, food services, exterminators, and every other conceivable service! *It takes a village to kill a child,* and we don't have to participate!

Priests for Life is ready to assist all who refuse to service abortion facilities, and we call upon the pastors of the Church to summon their people to conscientious objection.

Protected Speech

FOR years I have been preaching that the best way to defend our right to free speech is to exercise it without fear. Ironically, the same reason that the meaningless slogan "pro-choice" sounds so meaningful to Americans is also the very reason that pro-life people can successfully convey their message—that is, *we protect freedom*. There is no freedom to kill. But one of the key freedoms is to *express our message*—any message—no matter how disagreeable it might be to those who receive it.

We in the Church grossly underestimate and under-utilize the power of the pro-life message to confront and transform our culture. Just ask yourself for a moment where the pro-life message is being proclaimed to people who don't want to hear it. If someone in your community does not go to church and would never go to a public pro-life talk, how and where will they hear the message that abortion is violent and must be stopped?

Will they hear it if they go to a County Fair, by means of a pro-life booth where literature is distributed? Maybe, but not frequently enough.

How about on the street corners, where pro-life people can gather and distribute literature and hold signs? Well, here's where we become less American than the Constitution. We are perfectly free, legally and morally, to exercise this option. But we shoot ourselves in the foot. We tell ourselves it can't be done, long before anyone else tries to tell us. Either we're confused about its legality, or we don't want to "turn people off" (and this, essentially, is a judgment on them, because we presume that we know how well disposed their heart is to receive the message), or we think that we have to be popular to be successful (we think this whenever it has been too long since we've read the Acts of the Apostles).

Then, of course, we don't want to disturb children. I'm not talking here about graphic images of aborted babies. We are afraid to disturb them even with *words* about abortion, as I saw in a meeting where a Catholic parish and school rejected the idea of putting up a sign that says "Abortion Kills Children" because it might give the children nightmares. The irony is that at that very time, the first-graders in that same school had made and posted in the hallways drawings of skeletons and bottomless pits with the words "Drugs Kill." (You figure it out!)

A pro-abortion constitutional attorney in New York was recently offended by a banner towed by an airplane; the banner depicted an aborted baby. Yet she wrote in *Newsday* that there is no legal way to stop such activity. The Supreme Court has ruled time and time again that speech isn't truly free if people can't shock or offend you.

When pro-abortion people are defending our right to express our message more than we are exercising that right, something is wrong.

Victory Party

"DO not be afraid to go out on the streets and into public places like the first apostles, who preached Christ and the good news of salvation in the squares of cities, towns and villages."

Thus spoke Pope John Paul II on August 15, 1993, to the young people gathered in Denver for World Youth Day. The United States heard a strong echo of that message, for young and old alike to proclaim the Gospel of Life in public places from coast to coast thanks to a Supreme Court victory that came about on February 26, 2003 in the *Scheidler vs. NOW* case.

Joseph Scheidler, Director of the Pro-life Action League, has inspired activists for decades to take the pro-life message into the squares of cities, towns and villages. He has done so with such success that it has cut into the business profits of the killing centers. In the eyes of the National Organization for Women, this could not be tolerated. So in 1986, they took the activists to court, and tried to use the RICO (Racketeer Influenced and Corrupt Organizations) statutes against them. RICO laws were crafted to stop organized crime and drug trafficking, not the peaceful, non-violent intervention of those who are trying to save lives.

But in 2003, in an 8 to 1 ruling, the court said that RICO cannot be used against the pro-life activists, even if their activities deprived the abortion mills of business.

The favorable ruling, however, is only part one of the solution. Part two is that grassroots activists take up the mandate of the Court and the Pope, and fully utilize their First Amendment rights by organizing public prayer vigils, picketing, leafleting, street preaching, sidewalk counseling, and other demonstrations and marches from coast to coast.

The call to do exactly this was issued at the Bring America Back to Life rally and convention in Chicago on June 7, 2003. The atmosphere was reminiscent of the spirit of the Acts of the Apostles, where you read that the apostles did not sit around hoping people would come to them to be converted. Instead, they went to the people, who did not even know they needed the Gospel. Moreover, the apostles did not plan their activities in a risk-averse way, trying at every turn to avoid unpopularity, rejection, fines, or jail. Rather, they were impelled by the truth of Christ, and ready to pay any price for proclaiming it.

The First Amendment protects our ability to challenge the Culture of Death and its spokespersons. The law cannot forbid our speech just because others may find it disagreeable, offensive, or upsetting. Let's use this tool without fear as we carry out the late Pope's words, "Do not be afraid to break out of comfortable and routine modes of living in order to take up the challenge of making Christ known."

Reverse the Question

EVEN when we understand the dimensions of the abortion tragedy, which kills our youngest brothers and sisters in numbers larger than any disease, disaster, or war, we are often afraid to act.

We can gain courage, however, from the story of the Good Samaritan (Lk 10:25-37). On the road from Jerusalem to Jericho, a man fell in with robbers. A priest and a levite came by, but did not stop to help. Despite their knowledge of the Law and Prophets, they walked right by. Why?

One of the reasons may be that they were afraid. The road from Jerusalem to Jericho is a steep and dangerous road. At the time of Jesus, it had come to be known as the "Bloody Pass." Because of its numerous curves, it lends itself to attacks by robbers who can easily hide not too far from their victims. Perhaps the priest and levite who passed by that man asked themselves, "If I stop to help this man, what will happen to me? Maybe the robbers who attacked him are still here. Maybe they're hiding just around the bend. This is a dangerous road. I better keep going."

Sometimes we ask the same question. If I speak up too loudly about the victims of abortion, what will happen to me? Will I face persecution, will I encounter opposition, will I lose popularity if I get involved in a cause like this?

Priests sometimes ask the same question. If I preach about abortion, what will happen to me? What will happen to my parish, my effectiveness, my image? What legal troubles might I provoke?

Politicians sometimes ask the same question. If I say I am pro-life, what will happen to my votes, to my standing in the polls, to my chances in the election?

And then the Good Samaritan came along, and he reversed the question. He didn't ask, "If I help this man, what will happen to me?" The Good Samaritan asked, "If I do *not* help this man, what will happen to *him*?" And that's the question for us. If I do *not* address this evil, what will happen to the unborn? If I do *not* get involved, what will happen to those who are vulnerable, to those who are marginalized in our society, those who are oppressed, those who have no one to speak for them?

Dr. Martin Luther King, Jr. brought out this same lesson from this same parable on the night before he was assassinated. He called the people to a "dangerous unselfishness" as he rallied them to stand with the oppressed sanitation workers in Memphis. And in regard to himself, he declared that it didn't matter what happened to him; he just wanted to do God's will.

These words of holocaust survivor Elie Weisel sum it up well: "I swore never to be silent whenever and wherever human beings endure suffering and humiliation. We must always take sides. Neutrality helps the oppressor, never the victim. Silence encourages the tormentor, never the tormented."

Part II
The Arguments

The Unity of the Pro-life Movement

THE pro-life movement is composed of a stunning number and variety of groups large and small, spanning all ages, professions, creeds, and practically every other designation we can name. Literally thousands of groups are active in the United States alone.

One of the reasons for this wide variety is that the goal of the pro-life movement is so basic and fundamental: the preservation of life itself. Because life itself is prior to any other rights or traits, no matter how diverse they may be, it stands to reason that a cause that seeks to protect the right to life will find adherents across that wide and diverse spectrum of human interests. In this sense, the presence of so many groups is a good and healthy sign.

Another reason for the wide variety of groups is the nature of abortion. It is the intersection of many trends in ethics, medicine, law, psychology, sociology, religion, politics, and numerous other disciplines. Any one of the many dimensions of abortion can easily demand a lifetime of research and labor. I often wonder why some consider a focus on abortion alone to be a "narrow" focus. My experience is just the opposite. The range of intellectual, moral, and practical avenues which this problem opens seem endless. Therefore, there need to be different groups which address different dimensions of abortion: medical groups, religious groups, post-abortion groups, legal groups, youth groups, and so forth.

Yet while there is good reason for the diversity and number of pro-life groups, there is never a justification for disunity. By *disunity*, I mean a phenomenon whereby one group sees another as a threat rather than as an ally, as one to compete with rather than cooperate with, despite the fact that the ultimate goal, restoring protection for human life, is the same.

Did you ever stop and think that this is the same dynamic which, when it occurs between a mother and her preborn child, leads to abortion? Mom sees the child as a threat. She thinks the only road to her own fulfillment is to push the obstacle, the child, out of the way. Abortion rests on enmity where there should be welcome. That is true when the parties are mother and child; that is true when the parties are groups or organizations.

We end abortion when we help mom and dad to trust that the child is not an obstacle to their fulfillment. Rather, both child and parents find their fulfillment in giving themselves to each other in love.

The same is true among pro-life groups. Giving ourselves to each other in a dynamic trust and cooperation will overcome in us what we want pregnant mothers to overcome in their own minds and hearts. It is time for us to give them the example.

Pope John Paul II summed it up: "No single person or group has a monopoly on the defense and promotion of life. These are everyone's task and responsibility" (*Gospel of Life* #91).

Why We Can't "Agree to Disagree"?

THE solution that some propose to the divisive controversy over abortion is that the opposing parties in this dispute should simply "agree to disagree." This is presented as a reasonable option. It does not require that either side change its views, but simply agree to allow the different views, and the practices that flow from them.

Sorry, but this is a proposal we in the pro-life movement can't accept.

First of all, to ask us to "agree to disagree" about abortion is to ask us to change our position on it. Why, after all, do we disagree in the first place? When we oppose abortion, we disagree with the notion that it is even negotiable. We do not only claim that *we* cannot practice it, but that *nobody* can practice it, precisely because it violates the most fundamental human right, the right to life. To "agree to disagree" means that we no longer see abortion for what it is—a violation of a right so fundamental that disagreement cannot be allowed to tamper with it.

To "agree to disagree" is to foster the notion that the baby is a baby only if the mother thinks it is, that the child has value only if the mother says it does, and that we have responsibility only for those we choose to have responsibility for.

Certainly, there are many disputes in our nation about which we can "agree to disagree." Various proposals, programs, and strategies can be debated as we try to figure out how best to secure people's rights. But these legitimate areas of disagreement relate to *how* to secure people's rights, whereas the abortion controversy is about *whether* to secure or even recognize those rights at all. We can agree to disagree whether certain government programs should be allowed, but not whether acts of violence should be allowed. "Agree to disagree" seems like a neutral posture to assume, but it neutralizes what can never be neutral: the right to life itself.

Furthermore, the abortion dispute is not merely about conceptual disagreement. It's about justice. It's about violence, bloodshed, and victims who need to be defended. In the midst of a policy permitting 4,000 babies a day to be killed, to "agree to disagree" means to cease to defend the absolute rights of the victim.

We don't fight oppression by "agreeing to disagree" with the oppressor. It is precisely when the oppressor disagrees that we have to intervene to stop the violence. The fact that the oppressor does not recognize the victim as a person does not remove our obligation to the victim. In the face of injustice, we are not simply called to disagree with it, but to stop it.

The proposal to "agree to disagree" presumes the issue is about people disagreeing over abortion, not about people being killed by abortion. The proposal shows how invisible the unborn victim remains.

It is a false solution indeed.

Abortion Thinking Is Upside Down

IF anyone tells you the baby in the womb is not a baby, that person may as well tell you the earth is flat.

Pro-lifers have heard the out-of-date, unscientific assertion "It's not a baby" for many years. People who say this ought to be asked when are they going to catch up with the times. These are the days of fetoscopy and fetal surgery. Of course we know when life begins. And we know that the earth is not flat.

But now those who promote abortion say something even worse than "The earth is flat." They now essentially say, "The earth is flat if you think it's flat, and it's round if you think it's round. Decide for yourself." Whether the baby in the womb is a baby or not really doesn't matter to them, because its fate will depend on the mother's choice. Period.

This is the mentality we are dealing with. It was clearly expressed to me one day by a man holding a sign that said "Keep Baby-Killing Legal." He told me that he supports abortion and wants to be honest about what he is supporting. The value of the baby depends on the mother's choice.

Pro-lifers need to understand that this is how a growing number of pro-abortion people think. In dealing with this attitude, we need to point out several things.

People's decisions don't determine reality. I cannot even decide the weather. It should be even clearer that the moral value of a life cannot depend on my choice.

If the value of others' lives does depend on my choice, then all people are not equal. But our country was founded on the teaching that all people are equal, and that the weak should be protected from the strong.

If the value of a life depends on my choice, then so does the value of a lot of other things. If a mother can decide to kill her own child, then she can also decide to beat her own child, or cut off the child's hand, or torture the child. If, furthermore, a child's life depends on choice, then so does a house, a car, and a bank account. If baby-killing can be legal, why not car theft and bank robbery? "But those things are illegal," someone will say. So what? If the value of a life depends on my choice, so does the value of a law. The law has value if I say it does. Abortion is OK if I say it is. The earth is flat if I say it is.

It should be clear from this line of reasoning that the pro-abortion mentality turns civilization upside down, and produces a chaos that the pro-abortion people themselves will not want. The difference between them and us, of course, is that we see that more chaos necessarily follows in the wake of abortion. They say it follows only if they think it does.

Ask Questions

SO what do you do when your friend, relative, neighbor or co-worker says he or she is "pro-choice"?

A simple key to having a fruitful discussion with an abortion supporter is to *ask the person questions.* After all, you want the person to think, and a good question forces the other to think through his/her response. It also lets people know you are interested in what they really think, and in learning more about what they think and why they think it, you will be better able to lead them the right way. It is easy for others to decide that they do not want to listen to you. But it is much harder for them not to want *you to listen to them!* Everyone likes to be listened to. So ask some questions and listen! Once the other person knows you are listening to him/her, it helps to keep the conversation calm, and leads the exchange beyond the level of slogans.

It is amazing to see how shallow a person's position on abortion can be. People easily identify with nice-sounding slogans without really thinking through their position on the controversy. You will find out how true this is if you ask a person who identifies him/herself as "pro-choice" to explain the meaning of the phrase. "What does that mean?" Then stop, look at the person, and wait for a response. Here is a sample exchange, taken from an actual conversation:

a. *When it comes to abortion, I'm pro-choice.*

b. I see. Could you tell me what you mean by that?

a. *Well, a woman should be able to choose whether to continue her pregnancy.*

b. Well, in your opinion, how far into the pregnancy should she have that choice?

a. *She should decide.*

b. Yes, you are saying she should decide, but for how long?

a. *Well, it is better if she decides early rather than late.*

b. Why? What makes it better? And if it is, say, the seventh month, should she still be able to choose abortion?

Notice that in this exchange, the pro-lifer did not launch into an explanation of why "pro-choice" is a meaningless phrase, which it is, or of why freedom is subordinate to life itself, which it is, or even of what choosing an abortion actually does. What the prolifer is doing here is asking the pro-choicer to face up to his/her own position. *What does it mean? What position do you actually take?* If you go back over the brief exchange, you will see that this could even be a conversation between two "prochoicers," one of whom is simply trying to understand the other's position, which very well could be similar to his own. This approach is extremely valuable, because one cannot make you understand his position if he does not understand it himself, and to attempt to understand one's own position, when that position is wrong, can help one discover the truth.

Religious Beliefs, Abortion, and the Law

IN the many discussions I have with those who perform abortions, a very predictable pattern arises before long. I talk to them about science, and they talk to me about faith.

The pattern begins when I ask the question, "Does an abortion destroy a human life?" The answer I hear is, "I don't know when the child receives a soul." In one breath, the topic of discussion was an observable procedure from the perspective of verifiable science. In the next breath, the topic was spiritual and invisible: when do children receive souls?

This twist in the discussion is not limited to those who provide abortions. It also happens with many others who favor the availability of legal abortion. After all, they argue, since we have religious freedom in this country, people should be allowed to believe what they want about when the soul begins to exist. It would be wrong to impose by law one particular religious or theological position on this matter.

The truth is, however, that the pro-life movement does not seek to impose by law any religious or theological belief, whether about the soul or anything else. Such an effort is both misguided and unnecessary.

Suppose, for example, that I do not believe that you have a soul. Does that give me the right to kill you? No, it does not. Your life is still protected by the law, *despite my beliefs*. Does the law that protects your life require me to believe that you have a soul? No it does not. It doesn't even require me to believe that souls exist at all. What it requires is that *whatever I believe*, I refrain from taking your life. The law protects both the right to believe and the life of the believer.

That is what the pro-life movement wants. We are simply calling for the protection of all human beings.

We also uphold religious liberty, which means that religious beliefs should be embraced freely, not imposed by law. We also recognize that to invoke religious liberty to destroy another's life is an intolerable abuse.

If someone does not believe the child in the womb has a soul, that is his or her business. But to go on and say that *because* one doesn't believe that, it should be legal to kill the child, is equally as unjust as to say that because one doesn't believe you have a soul, it should be legal to kill you. The law doesn't care about the *belief*; it regulates the *action*.

The law's criterion for who receives protection should be the verifiable evidence of science, rather that the subjective criterion of religious belief. There is such a thing as religious *truth*. But whether a baby lives or dies should not depend on whether or not everyone in society has acknowledged that truth. Human life needs protection *now*. The freedom "not to believe" should never be confused with freedom to destroy others.

Persons

THE 14th amendment to the Constitution states in part, "nor shall any State deprive any person of life, liberty, or property without due process of law; nor deny to any person within its jurisdiction the equal protection of the laws." The fact that the law does not protect children in the womb from abortion is rooted in the words of the 1973 *Roe vs. Wade* decision, "the word *person* as used in the Fourteenth Amendment does not include the unborn."

What is less widely known is the decision handed down eight months before *Roe vs. Wade*, in which personhood was also discussed in relation to protecting the environment. In the decision, *Sierra Club vs. Morton*, Justice Douglas argued in the following words:

"The ordinary corporation is a 'person' for purposes of the adjudicatory process. . . . So it should be as respects valleys, alpine meadows, rivers, lakes, estuaries, beaches, ridges, groves of trees, swampland, or even air that feels the destructive pressures of modern technology and modern life . . . With all respect, the problem is to make certain that the inanimate objects, which are the very core of America's beauty, have spokesmen before they are destroyed. . . . The voice of the inanimate object, therefore, should not be stilled. . . . That is why these environmental issues should be tendered by the inanimate object itself. Then there will be assurances that all of the forms of life which it represents will stand before the court—the pileated woodpecker as well as the coyote and bear, the lemmings as well as the trout in the streams. Those inarticulate members of the ecological group cannot speak. . . ."

Eight months later, he ruled with the majority in *Roe vs. Wade* that "the word *person* . . . does not include the unborn."

There is a stunning arbitrariness to this decision, and a stunning implication about the power of the government. To support *Roe vs. Wade* is not merely to allow the existence of the most common surgical procedure in America. It is to acknowledge that the government has the power to say who is a person and who is not. And *if the government is to have that say,* then who is to limit the groups to whom it is applied?

Supporters of *Roe vs. Wade* can ask, "Could the government ever declare my teenage daughter to be a non-person? Could it ever say I am not a person?" If the answer is no, then such a person has not understood the full implication of *Roe vs. Wade.*

Such supporters say the government "should not be involved in the abortion decision." How true! In fact, the government got too involved in it when, in 1973, it presumed to have the power to deprive some of the right to live! The government should indeed back away from the abortion decision by recognizing that it does not have the power to permit the lives of the innocent to be taken.

Those who govern are to govern *all* the people. *All* includes the smallest and weakest, the *persons* yet unborn.

A Poll of the Polls

PROFESSOR Raymond J. Adamek (Department of Sociology, Kent State University) has done the pro-life movement a great service in his study "Abortion Polls 1965-1998: Designed to Measure or to Mold Public Opinion?"

His analysis of major opinion polls on the abortion question during that time frame reveals that, given the way the questions are asked, what is being measured is *not* the public's opinion about the current abortion laws and practice. What is being measured is their opinion about *imaginary* abortion laws and practice. This is simply because so many of the questions misrepresent the facts.

Professor Adamek explains, "On 85 occasions from 1973 to 1998, 8 major pollsters described *Roe v. Wade* as permitting abortion during 'the first three months of pregnancy.' . . . [T]his description is incomplete and misleading, since it gives the uninformed respondent the impression that the Court did not legalize abortion beyond the first trimester, and focuses the attention of the informed respondent on only part of the decision."

A reading of *Roe* and subsequent abortion decisions, a study of the legislation and Court battles on partial-birth abortion, or a journey through the "A" section of the Yellow Pages of a major city is enough to dispel any doubts that abortion is legal throughout pregnancy. So why can't a poll that wants to measure what people think about that policy ask people what they think about that policy, instead of what they think about some *different* policy?

The conclusion: You simply can't believe a poll that tells you that most Americans agree with *Roe vs. Wade*.

They still don't know what the decision said, and it is most likely that the pollster hasn't helped them find out.

Another imbalance in abortion poll questions is the way they speak about "rights." Professor Adamek explains that he analyzed "all questions from 1965 through 1998 that explicitly mentioned the woman or the unborn and the word 'right(s)'. . . . An illustrative 'woman's right' question is: Do you favor or oppose the Supreme Court ruling that women have the right to have an abortion during the first three months of their pregnancy? (*Yankelovich Clancy Shulman*, 4/5/89). We found 66 items asking about the woman's right to (choose) abortion but none asking exclusively about the unborn's right to life! By asking questions about only one side of the rights issue, polls yield an incomplete and skewed picture of public opinion."

A third problem area is the fact that 65% of questions referred to the abortion-making decision as one in which the doctor was involved. Yet in reality, fewer than 25% of women, if that many, bring the doctor into the decision-making process at all. Now since the majority of Americans approve medical necessity as a justification for abortion, mentioning the doctor in the question increases the "pro-choice" responses. Questions which specify the actual reasons for which abortions occur would yield a better measure of what people think about abortion practice in America.

Good practical advice, therefore: Don't just look at a poll's results; *look at its questions.*

Persuading People that Rape Does Not Justify Abortion

"**W**ELL what about rape? Are you saying that woman can't have an abortion?"

Normally, the primary concern of this question is not, *Do you think abortion is OK in this instance?*, despite the fact that this is how the question may be expressed. The concern which is uppermost for the questioner is, *Don't you care about this woman? Won't you have compassion and help her?*

When we answer the question, therefore, let's start by addressing this point head on. Before we even mention abortion, we should stress that we agree totally that the woman who has been raped has undergone a terrible trauma, which we can hardly begin to understand, and that her well-being is very much our concern. Stress this point strongly, and go further by saying that we in the pro-life movement are ready to reach out to such women, giving them counsel, healing, and compassion.

This approach, of course, differs in that it does not start where most people would start in answering this challenge: namely, with the rights of the child. It starts with concern for the woman, which is where the questioner is.

Then, having agreed that the woman has been victimized and needs our help, you can frame the question of abortion in this manner: *Will an abortion help her?* By asking this, you are now questioning what is normally an unspoken, unchallenged assumption, namely, that the abortion is somehow a solution to the rape, and somehow helps alleviate the pain and trauma of the woman.

Having questioned this assumption, next bring in the evidence that not only does the abortion *not alleviate* the trauma of the rape, but it brings *a trauma of its own*. Countless women suffer for years and decades after abortion. I know of women who have been raped and then had abortions, and are in counseling not for the rape but for the abortion! In rape, the trauma is "Someone hurt me." In abortion, the trauma is "I hurt and killed someone else: my child." That brings even more grief.

We therefore help the questioner to see that our reason for denying the rape victim an abortion is not based on insensitivity but rather on compassion, that is, the same basis on which the questioner is challenging us to allow the abortion.

The next step of the process is to show that our compassion actually is more inclusive than that of those who would allow abortion. Having established that we care about the rape victim, we then ask the powerful questions, Why can't we love them both? Why can't we extend to the child the same practical compassion which we both agree belongs to the woman? Why can't we expand the boundaries of those we welcome and care for? Why should helping and loving one (the mom) mean destroying the other (the child)? In reality, you cannot help one without helping the other and you cannot hurt one without hurting the other.

Abortion for Men

ONE of the slogans used by extremists in the pro-abortion movement is, "If men could get pregnant, abortion would be a sacrament." The slogan, besides being simply ignorant, is an insult to the Church and to the integrity of pro-life people. Less crude expressions of the same sentiment take shape in arguments like, "The prohibition of abortion discriminates against women," and "Pro-life people are intent on depriving women of their rights." In fact, pro-abortion forces took this argument all the way to the Supreme Court, but lost in their attempt to claim that women as a class were discriminated against by pro-life efforts.

The fact is that we oppose abortion both for women *and* for men. The fact that men do not get pregnant does not stop them from *choosing abortion*. Indeed, anyone who has worked directly to stop abortions has seen many instances in which the "choice" in question was being made by the man, *not* by the woman. In the thousands of case testimonies I have in my office, time after time I read these or similar words: "My boyfriend wanted me to have the abortion; I was unsure," or "The baby's father said that unless I aborted the child, he would leave."

Of course. Abortion is not about women's rights. It is often about men wanting the right to be able to continue to have sexual relations without the "intrusive burden" of the child that can come about.

Morally speaking, the sin of abortion is committed *when it is chosen, knowingly and willingly.* Many factors mitigate the guilt, but the point here is that the *choosing of abortion* does not require that one be pregnant. Men choose abortion; men perform abortions. Men are therefore often guilty of the sin of abortion.

Being pro-life is in no way to single out *women* for blame. Being pro-life is about helping men and women alike to have the courage to do what is right, namely, to conceive children only within the bounds of valid marriage, and to protect all children who have been conceived under any circumstances.

Ministry to men is increasingly important, and Christians are responding more and more. We see movements like Promise Keepers, St. Joseph's Covenant Keepers, and the Catholic Men's Fellowship striving to meet the pastoral needs of men in our day. We also see the post-abortion movement increasingly extending its resources of counseling and healing to the men who have become entrapped in the lie that abortion is a solution to their problems.

It was the promoters of abortion who from the beginning framed abortion as simply a "woman's issue." But, abortion involves everyone. Once, at a Life Chain, I was asked by a passerby what right I had, as a man, to say anything about abortion. "I'm a human being," I replied, "and when my fellow human beings are being killed, I have a right to stand up and say no." "No," that is, whether it is addressed to a woman or to a man.

Experience

WHETHER it's from a legislator opposing restrictions on abortion, or a pro-abortion activist at a demonstration, one of the most common objections voiced against those who would eliminate abortion is, "Who are you to tell this woman she can't have an abortion? You do not know what it's like to be pregnant, nor can you judge her personal experience in the midst of this crisis. Only she knows what she is going through, and therefore only she can decide."

Here are a few suggested ways to respond.

First of all, those who advocate against abortion are mostly women, vast numbers of whom have been through the very experiences of crisis pregnancy that pro-abortion activists claim pro-life people don't know. Moreover, many of them also know the experience of having an abortion—the very bitter experience which, if experience is an argument at all, is one of the strongest arguments against abortion that there can ever be. One of the many blind spots of the pro-abortion movement is precisely that it downplays the experience of those who suffer from abortion, even decades after they have had the "simple" procedure.

Secondly, it is noteworthy that the ability to experience pregnancy only seems to be required for those who speak *against* abortion, not for those who speak *for it.* Among the latter would be the men who are former Presidents, Supreme Court Justices, legislators and activists who fight hard and speak loud about "upholding the right to choose." And, of course, don't forget the fathers and boyfriends who tell the girl that she has to have an abortion, even over her objections, because they "know what is best" in that situation.

Thirdly, experience is not the only factor to consider in evaluating whether a particular activity should be allowed or prohibited in society and law. I have never experienced the personal pressures a crisis pregnancy brings. But neither have I experienced the personal pressures which would lead a parent to abuse her children, nor the psychological twists and turns of the drug addict, or of the latest person to rob a bank. What is going on within them, to lead them to such actions? I have not experienced it.

Am I therefore to be silent about their actions?

Some choices have victims, and when somebody's choice destroys somebody else's life, the experience of the chooser is not the most relevant factor. The most relevant factor is the protection of the lives and rights of those around him or her. The fact that we do not have the same experience should make us compassionate, and motivate us to strive to understand the person. But it brings no obligation to permit destructive activity.

A final word on experience. With more and more studies showing the likelihood of fetal pain, and with greater awareness of the brutality of abortion procedures, is it not appropriate to also consider the experience of the baby who is aborted? Experience, indeed, cuts both ways.

September 11 and Abortion

A NUMBER of commentators since September 11, 2001 have carefully drawn the comparison between the acts of terrorism that occurred on that day and the daily terrorism of abortion. Both are attacks on innocent human life.

Another link between the two is *the perversion of religion*.

Priests for Life maintains excellent working relationships with Muslims, and the people who work with us could never imagine a God who would justify people taking innocent human life. Yet we have learned that there are people in the world who call upon the one they regard as the world's Creator, and thank Him for the successful destruction of some of His creatures.

"You shall not use the Name of the Lord your God in vain." That commandment does not simply forbid using God's name as a curse word. It forbids invoking God to justify evil acts. It forbids thanking God for what happened on September 11.

The name of God is also taken in vain to justify abortion. Many supporters of the killing of innocent babies engage in the same kind of perversion of religion.

If you want proof, start by looking at the website www.rcrc.org. It is the Religious Coalition for Reproductive Choice. A more accurate title for the group would be False Prophets. They take the name of Jesus Christ, and His saving Gospel, and try to find there a justification for the dismemberment of tiny children.

The logo on their website is, "We are pro-choice *because* of our faith."

They even have a Clergy for Choice Network. The "Clergy for Choice Pledge" reads in part, "We clergy members, representing many different religious denominations around the country, pledge our strong support for reproductive choice, which encompasses access to safe, reliable contraception, family planning education, comprehensive sexuality education, affordable and reliable childcare and health care, adoption services, and access to safe, legal, and affordable abortions."

If you still doubt that abortion involves an explicit perversion of religion, read the cover story in the October 1993 issue of *New Age Journal* ("Sister Against Sister," p.66). Author Brenda Peterson writes, "In her book *Pagan Meditations*, Ginette Paris describes abortion as an essentially religious act, a sacred sacrifice to Artemis. 'One aborts an impossible love,' she writes, 'not a hatred.' In her new book, *The Sacrament of Abortion*, Paris explains further that if we saw abortion as a sacred ritual, it would restore to the act a sense of the sanctity of life."

Newsweek magazine reports (October 17, 1994) that many abortionists "have a missionary sense about their work." Dr. Curtis Boyd, a Texas abortionist, told the magazine, "I perform abortions *because* of my religion." Dr. Boyd is often asked by Native American women to bless the aborted fetus, and by Catholic women to baptize it. He proposes schools of theology develop special ceremonies and prayers to mark the loss of a fetus.

You shall not use the name of the Lord in vain—neither for terrorism against the born or the unborn.

A Unique Poverty

IN *Living the Gospel of Life,* our bishops describe abortion as a *preeminent* threat to human dignity. One of the reasons, they point out, is that it is committed against *the weakest and most defenseless.*

It is obvious that these children cannot speak for themselves. They cannot organize a "movement," and they *can't even pray.* After all, if someone is attacked and unable to call for help, he or she can still pray. The unborn can't.

Yet there is another aspect to the *weakness,* the *poverty* of the unborn that deserves more attention. It is a *weakness in their ability to make a psychological impact* on us.

When teens are shot in schools, or people die in an airline disaster, or troops go into war, prayer services are held all over the place. Petitions appear in the General Intercessions at Mass, and expressions of concern appear in the bulletin . . . as they should.

Yet when the same number of babies are killed by abortion every few minutes, there is no comparison in the reaction. Instead, in some quarters, objections are raised about even mentioning the fact.

Where is the disconnect here?

Part of this problem, despite the advancement of imaging techniques that introduce us to the unborn, is "out of sight, out of mind." But the problem is even deeper. Much of it has to do with the dynamics of pain and denial. Some of it has to do with how we respond to moral values.

On a moral level, we can acknowledge readily enough that *all human beings are equal* and that, in this sense, the *taking of a human life* is as much of a tragedy in one situation as in another. Considering *the moral good being attacked*—*human life*—the age of the human being does not make a difference.

But psychologically, there is a big difference, and the unborn are on the losing end of the deal. While their death will have a devastating impact on the mother and father (and others in the family) who will experience some form of post-abortion distress, *Why, nevertheless, does their death make less of an impact on us and on society overall?*

Well, we haven't yet named them or heard their voices. There are no memorable experiences we have shared with them, or bonds of friendship that make their passing so hard to take. Except maybe for some ultrasounds, we have not seen them. Nor have we begun to experience the special, unique features of the personality of each one, or the early signs of the promising contributions they can make to society and history. Because of all this, their loss has less of an emotional price tag.

Here, then, is the challenge for us: Will we respond to the destruction of a moral good *based primarily on its psychological aspect* or rather based primarily *on its moral aspect?*

If the former, then the destruction of the unborn will continue to receive less attention than the (morally equivalent) destruction of their older brothers and sisters.

Winning the War on Images

THE battle to restore protection to our preborn brothers and sisters is in many ways a war of words, and a lot of effort has been invested in the pro-life movement to teach people how to win the war of words. There are, in the end, a limited number of slogans and arguments used by the defenders of abortion, and every one of these verbal weapons can be readily counteracted by the truth that the pro-life position contains. Ultimately, there is no way to rationally defend the killing of little babies.

Defenders of abortion have actually known this for a long time, and therefore have taken the offensive by using the power of images to appeal to the emotions of the audience and overpower the reasoning process. Take a simple example. Since 1995, much public attention has been given to the partial-birth abortion procedure as federal and state legislation was introduced to ban it. Medically accurate diagrams of this procedure were shown in the halls of Congress and on national television, to the rightful disgust of the vast majority of decent people. The defenders of this procedure could not deny that it was real, and could not rationally defend it. Their strategy was discussed in a seminar at a national meeting of the National Abortion Federation: instead of focusing on the procedure, focus on heart-wrenching cases of women who allegedly needed this procedure to preserve their life, health, and fertility. Read their testimonies, show pictures of them and their other live, healthy children, and get the public to feel their grief.

This very strategy was evident both on the floor of Congress and also at the White House when President

Clinton vetoed the ban in the presence of women who allegedly suffered such hard cases.

The power of the image is great. And it is not a power that should be reserved to defenders of abortion. We can use it just as effectively.

What, then, would be a powerful pro-life image to counteract that used to defend partial-birth abortion? The image of the moms who faced medically complicated pregnancies and bravely brought their children to birth is a perfect antidote. During the efforts to ban partial-birth abortion, a number of such women have made their stories known. In fact, they sought an audience with President Clinton, but he refused to meet with them. The pro-life movement must pick up the slack, and give a voice to the heroic parents who gave life in such difficult circumstances.

We should not be afraid to pull the heartstrings of America in defense of life! This is not manipulation. It is, rather, giving a face and a feel to the truth we express in our propositions! Let those who have bravely chosen life in traumatic circumstances, and want to share their story, be given a hearing in the media, in our legislatures, in our churches! Most of all, may we continue to give them a place in our hearts for all they have done to strengthen the rest of us to defend life!

The Evil of Contraception

SINCE *Roe vs. Wade,* there have been three versions of the "Pastoral Plan for Pro-life Activities" issued by the US Catholic Bishops. The latest came out in November, 2001. In this third version, for the first time, the connection between abortion and contraception is explicitly discussed.

There are many aspects to this connection. First of all, some contraceptives cause abortions, and hence are not contraceptives at all. It is critical, moreover, to understand—as Pope John Paul II pointed out in *The Gospel of Life*—that abortion and contraception are *specifically different evils that differ in nature and gravity.* Abortion takes a human life; contraception distorts the meaning of human sexuality. Both are *always* morally wrong.

Contraception, strictly considered as *preventing fertilization,* is one of many factors leading to an increase of abortion in our world. As the bishops write, ". . . [S]ome promote widespread use of contraception as a means to reduce abortions and even criticize the Church for not accepting this approach. It is noteworthy that as acceptance and use of contraception have increased in our society, so have acceptance and use of abortion. Couples who unintentionally conceive a child while using contraception are far more likely to resort to abortion than others."

As Fr. Paul Marx, OSB, and I often discussed, there is no culture or subculture in the world that has permitted contraception and then has not gone on to permit abortion.

The ultimate root of the evil of contraception is that it denies that God is God. The attitude behind it is, "I am the one who ultimately decides whether a human being will come into the world."

As a result of that attitude, one thinks he or she can then *change the meaning of sexual intimacy* by holding back its life-giving power. Obviously, the same activity by which people express the deepest physical intimacy also can give rise to a new life. Did you ever wonder why God put these two aspects together in the same action? Could He not have invented one action to express love and intimacy, and another, separate action to bring about new life? Is it an accident that both belong to the same act, or did God run out of ideas?

Neither, of course. God acted with a deliberate and wise plan in creating human sexuality. His plan says that when one human being gives him/herself totally to another, *that total "yes" includes a "yes" to new life.* The partners put themselves in a stance of readiness. "Lord of my life and my body, in giving my body to another, I give my fertility, and I accept my partner's fertility. I am ready to accept Your gift. Now I leave it up to You, my Lord, as to whether You will actually give that gift at this time."

As Dr. Bernard Nathanson explains, it is not that contraception causes abortion; rather, both are caused by *the perversion of autonomy*—taking freedom and using it to stop rather than to welcome life.

Wishful Thinking

IF you want some good examples of wishful thinking, ask abortion-rights advocates what they think chemical abortion methods like RU-486 will do to the abortion debate. They will use such expressions as "the triumph of medicine over politics" and "the removal of the abortion issue from public demonstrations." They go so far as to claim that the consequent privatization of the procedure will mean that the pro-life movement will not be able to oppose it.

My response to them is "Dream on . . ."

First of all, chemical abortion can never fully or even mostly replace surgical abortion. Chemical abortion kills babies only in the earliest weeks of pregnancy, and the very ambivalence that surrounds pregnancy and abortion in the minds and emotions of so many girls accounts for the delay that leads to abortions later in pregnancy.

Another factor, reflected in statistics from countries that have offered RU-486 for years, is that most who have abortions prefer surgical methods because they do not want powerful synthetic steroids, with their largely unknown long-term effects, messing up their bodies.

The provision of the chemical technique, furthermore, with its multiple visits to abortion centers, hardly privatizes it.

But let's get more to the heart of the matter. Even if abortion were totally privatized by chemical methods, the mission—and opportunity—of the pro-life movement would not change in the least. If those who are pregnant can find out who administers chemical abortions, then so can the pro-life movement, and the pro-life movement will be there to protest the providers and provide alternatives for the mothers. Just as doctors who destroy babies and their mothers by surgical methods are increasingly brought to court to account for their malpractice, so will doctors who destroy babies and their mothers by chemical methods.

Why does the abortion-rights movement think that by changing their methods of injustice, we will stop crying out for justice? What makes them imagine that by coming up with new ways to kill children, they can make us stop loving those children and working to save them?

No matter the method of abortion, fundamental questions will still cry out for answers: Who are the unborn? Are they equal in dignity to the born? Who is responsible for them? Will they be protected and welcomed in a land which declares that all are created equal? Why should the rightful advancement of women—which we support—depend on providing them with license to kill their children?

Instead of devising new ways to kill, why don't those who support abortion join hands with those who oppose abortion in order to devise new ways to provide for mothers, fathers, and children, especially in difficult circumstances?

To those, then, who prematurely claim victory as they herald chemical abortion methods, *you are dreaming*. And to those who work to advance the right to life, *stay the course, and carry on with joy your mission, which can never grow old!*

There Are No Exceptions

"THIS is my blood . . . It will be shed for you and for all. . ." (cf. Mt 26:28).

These words of the Lord Jesus indicate His universal will for salvation. He died for each and every human being who ever existed and ever will exist.

Furthermore, it was through Him that they were made. "Without Him there was nothing" (Jn 1:3). "All things were created through Him and for Him" (Col 1:16).

The love of God has no exceptions; the command He gives us to love one another likewise admits of no exceptions. "Love one another as I have loved you" (Jn 15:12). The Christian is not free to discriminate, or to exclude anyone from his or her love. Such exclusion is incompatible with the love of God Himself. This is the basis for saying that *no* innocent human life may ever be deliberately destroyed; this is the root and source of the unchanging truth that *no abortion is ever justified*.

Abortion is, according to the teaching of the Church, an *intrinsic evil*. It is evil by its very nature, and that evil is not altered by circumstances. To put it another way, if one lived for a million years—or forever—and did nothing but try to imagine circumstances that could justify a single abortion, one could never imagine one. It simply does not exist.

Every abortion, no matter what the circumstances, contradicts the law and will of God.

The circumstances in which a child is conceived— whether they were planned or not, whether they were the embrace of spousal love or the violent act of rape or incest—can never make an abortion morally permissible.

The circumstances in which the pregnancy advances—whether the health or life of the mother is threatened or not, or whether her social or economic situation is extremely grave—can never justify the direct killing of a child.

Human law, furthermore, can never justify a single act of abortion. There is no Court, King, Governor, President, Parliament, or Prince anywhere on earth or any time in history who can issue any decision, decree or declaration that would justify even a single abortion. When human lawmakers attempt to do so, the "law" that results is not simply a bad law; *it is, in fact, no law at all, and carries neither authentic juridical validity nor any obligation to obey it.*

Life can be confusing, and the temptation to compromise with evil can be great. But the teaching about abortion is as clear and direct as it can be, and is best summed up with one word: *never.*

Part III
The Women

The Perfect Message

ONE of the common concerns priests have in regard to speaking about abortion is that they don't want to hurt the women in the congregation who have had abortions. They feel that the presence of such women is a reason to be silent about it.

Just the opposite is true, however. Experts in post-abortion syndrome tell us that the first step toward healing is to break out of denial, and silence does not help to do that. Silence motivated by the best of intentions, moreover, does not interpret itself. The woman suffering from abortion may think we are silent because we do not know her pain, do not care, or have no hope to offer. In truth, however, we speak because we do know, do care, and do offer hope.

There are two things that the post-abortive woman does *not* need to hear.

One is, "It's no big deal." In reality, she knows abortion is a big deal and experiences a natural grief for her child who has been killed. Yet many in society make her feel silly for feeling sad. Her grief, therefore, cannot be adequately expressed and processed. The process is short-circuited.

Moreover, she may well be quite angry with those whose message about "no big deal" got her into the mess of abortion in the first place. To hear that message again, and to be given more excuses, is the last thing she needs.

The second thing the post-abortive woman does *not* need is someone who will condemn her and drive her deeper into the despair which the act of abortion is all too capable of generating on its own.

Our message, the message of the Church and of the pro-life movement, holds exactly the right balance. Our clear identification of abortion as an evil which is never morally licit corresponds with the deepest truth she is hearing in her mind and heart. It cuts through the rhetoric, empty excuses, and terrible pressures others have heaped upon her. It breaks through denial and assures her she has a reason for her grief.

Then, at the same time and in the same breath, we give the message of hope. The doors of the Church are open. We are not here to reject or condemn, but to welcome back to the peace and mercy of Christ whoever has been involved in abortion. I even know of someone who had 24 abortions. Even she can be forgiven. We long to welcome her back. So does God.

The process of healing is delicate and long. Sometimes it begins with pain. The availability of compassionate post-abortion counselors in the community goes a long way.

I always recall the words of the post-abortive woman who, after a pro-life homily I gave, said to me, "Father, I have pain when I hear about abortion. . . . But please, please keep preaching about it, because it consoles me greatly to know that through that homily, someone could be spared the whole journey of grief I have had to go through."

Indeed, let us speak.

Rachel's Vineyard

"I CANNOT think of another work of this kind so well done," Fr. Benedict Groeschel has written of Rachel's Vineyard. "A most difficult and painful human problem is engaged with faith, psychological insight and trust."

Having been involved for years in these retreats for people wounded by abortion, I could not agree more with that assessment. That is why I was so pleased when Theresa and Kevin Burke, the founders of Rachel's Vineyard, approached me with the request that this retreat program come under the umbrella of Priests for Life. As such, it is now becoming even better known by the priests of the nation and provides yet another way for them to extend the healing power of Christ through the Sacrament of Penance, through counseling, and through preaching. Moreover, the Rachel's Vineyard retreat can also be conducted in an ecumenical format, allowing Christians of all denominations to take part in a way that is consistent with their own background.

Rachel's Vineyard is a weekend retreat experience for women and men who have lost children through abortion. With the assistance of counselors and clergy, they explore the emotional and spiritual pain of their abortion in the presence of the Lord and in a confidential and supportive atmosphere. Because the wound of abortion is compounded by its secrecy and in fact consists of a destructive isolation of the individual, the person on the retreat finds a new freedom by sharing his or her pain with the others on the retreat, who have all had similar experiences, and benefits from their understanding, acceptance, and additional insight.

One of the most powerful and unique aspects to the retreat is the use of "Living Scriptures." This is essentially a group reflection on various scriptural events, utilizing a traditional method of meditation on Scripture by which a person imagines himself present at the event and involved in it. But instead of having this reflection within oneself and only in thought, the group dramatizes it together, again utilizing a very traditional Catholic approach, namely, using signs, symbols, and gestures to make spiritual realities more tangible. A simple example of this is the healing of Bartimaeus in chapter 10 of Mark's Gospel. At Rachel's Vineyard, the passage is read in the presence of all; the priest then goes to each person, along with a team member, who says, "Have courage, he is calling you." The person says, "Jesus, Son of David, have pity on me." The priest then says Jesus' words, "What do you want me to do for you?" The person then makes her request, in her own words. The priest bestows an individual blessing.

Thousands of Rachel's Vineyard retreats are taking place around the United States and around the world. Many dioceses have officially adopted this program for their abortion healing ministry. As more and more people come forward, breaking out of their guilt and shame-filled isolation, let us together welcome them to the Vineyard of the Church!

See www.RachelsVineyard.org for additional information.

Multiple Abortions

YOU have probably heard the statistic that almost half of the abortions that occur each day in America are *repeat abortions*. In other words, almost every other woman walking into an abortion mill has had the procedure before.

But *how many times* before?

Of the abortions reported in 1999 to the Centers for Disease Control (CDC), 26.2% of women who aborted had experienced one previous abortion; 11.2% had *two* previous abortions, and 7.5% had *three or more* previous abortions. The situation may be even worse than this, because the reports that states make to the CDC are voluntary, and the largest abortion state, California, does *not* report. Forty-six states do report, and this led to a total count of 861,789 legal induced abortions in 1999. That means that in one year, by the most conservative data available, 64,634 abortions were performed on women *who had had three or more previous abortions*. In 2000 the CDC reported that 18% of abortions were performed on women seeking *at least* their *third* termination.

Why would a woman have multiple abortions?

Several factors can account for this. Dr. Philip Ney points out that pregnancy, like sleep, is a *biorhythm*. If you are awakened in the middle of the night, your body says, *"Go back to sleep."* Many who abort, therefore, feel the urge to get pregnant again. A biorhythm has been interrupted. Many want a "replacement" or "atonement" baby.

Yet once pregnant again, they realize (or someone else *makes them realize*) that the same circumstances that led to the first abortion are still in place. Hence, another abortion follows. Often the mother, pregnant the second time, thinks, "I aborted my first child. I'm not worthy of being a mother. I don't deserve this child." And she goes to the abortion mill. Repeat abortions are a sign of ambivalence, and at times of self-punishment.

Dr. Theresa Burke also explains, "Repeat abortions and replacement pregnancies are two common ways in which women reenact elements of their abortion trauma" (*Forbidden Grief*, p.110). As Dr. Ney puts it, "Tragedy is repeated not because we do not understand, but because we are trying to understand" (*Deeply Damaged*, p.118). In other words, an underlying conflict, perhaps created by a previous trauma, is unresolved. We find we cannot resolve it by simply replaying it in our minds. *So we re-live it.* This happens in many arenas of life. The sexually abused child may become seductive; the child who lacked touch and affection may seek an emotionally cold partner, and so forth. We repeat what we don't understand, in the hopes of mastering it.

Repeat abortions can be repulsive even to people who call themselves "pro-choice" and even to those who work in abortion mills. Sometimes our own reaction is an exasperated, indignant, "How can she do that??!!" But we should change the question and ask instead, "How can I help you to heal?" That question expresses the heart of the pro-life movement, a movement that knows that the destiny of mother and child are forever intertwined, and that we can't love one without loving the other.

Let the healing begin.

Solidarity with Women

"SOLIDARITY with Women" is the effort of Priests for Life to respond to the call that Pope John Paul II made when he writes in *Crossing the Threshold of Hope,* "Therefore, in firmly rejecting 'pro choice' it is necessary to become courageously 'pro woman,' promoting a choice that is truly in favor of women . . . The only honest stance . . . is that of radical solidarity with the woman" (p.206-207). Likewise, in *Evangelium Vitae 99,* the Holy Father called for a *"new feminism"* whose purpose is *"to acknowledge and affirm the true genius of women in every aspect of the life of society, and overcome all discrimination, violence and exploitation."*

Through its "Solidarity with Women" effort, Priests for Life has faithfully reflected this call of the Holy Father, and this inherent demand of being pro-life. In thousands of parishes around the nation over the past decade, the priests of our organization have preached, and have trained countless other priests to preach the following theme: To be pro-life is to be pro-woman. We do not say, "Love the baby and forget about the mother." Rather, we say, "Why can't we love them both?" We can and we must. To harm one is to harm the other; to love and serve one is to love and serve the other.

"Pro-woman" is not simply a project, strategy, or package for the pro-life message. Rather, *it is that message.* Whenever someone speaks up for the equal dignity of the unborn child, that person is advancing the status of women. Whenever someone reveals the horror of abortion, that person is counteracting the exploitation of women, so many of whom are deceived into thinking that abortion is no horror at all. Whenever the pro-life message is advanced, women are ennobled.

"Solidarity with Women" involves multiple projects. For instance, our TV, radio, and print ads reveal how women are deceived, exploited, and killed by the abortion industry. Our *Defending Life* program continues to be the platform for countless women to speak to hundreds of millions of people worldwide about their pain and healing after abortion. Our website carries the largest collection of post-abortion testimonies on the internet (www.priestsforlife.org/postabortion). For years, we have called upon pastors to place as a permanent item on their parish bulletin cover the phone numbers for local alternatives to abortion.

One of our latest efforts is to co-sponsor the "Silent No More Awareness Campaign" on the internet (www.SilentNoMoreAwareness.org). Throughout the country, women who have found healing after their abortion are speaking out, revealing abortion for the harmful, empty promise that it is. In June 2003, we brought such women before a special gathering of members of the US House of Representatives in Washington. We will continue to give them opportunities to speak out from coast to coast.

This is a task for everyone, women and men alike. The basis of our solidarity with women, as well as with unborn children, is our common humanity, not our gender. Indeed, let us all speak and act *in solidarity with women!*

Silent No More

A BUSE victims often use the phrase "Silent No More" to indicate their response to being victimized. It may be surprising to some in our society, therefore, that more than three decades after the abortion decisions *Roe vs. Wade* and *Doe vs. Bolton*, that women from coast to coast are uniting under the banner of "Silent No More" because they have had abortions.

Not illegal ones in "back alleys"—which is more propaganda than reality—but legal ones in federally protected "clinics."

These women do not consider themselves freed, empowered, or ennobled because of their abortion. Rather, they testify that they were enslaved, weakened, and wounded. They were, in short, given a false promise, which is the essence of all temptation. They were told that this "procedure" would solve their problems. Instead, it brought more problems than they care to think about, namely, the whole range of physical and psychological wounds often described by the term "post-abortion syndrome."

What are these women doing this year that is different from what they have done over the past 33 years?

In our nation's Capitol and in cities across the country, they gather publicly at rallies and prayer events and hold signs that say, "I Regret My Abortion." Following the annual March for Life, the women assemble on the steps of the Supreme Court, on the very date, January 22, that abortion was legalized in 1973.

This campaign is being sponsored by NOEL (the pro-life outreach of Episcopalians) and Priests for Life.

But why do this? If abortion is so painful, some will ask, why make a public display out of one's experience?

The answer is understood only if one knows how shameful and painful the silence of abortion is. The grief that follows abortion is, in the words of Dr. Theresa Burke, a *"forbidden grief."* The grief is not acknowledged; it is not validated. People don't send sympathy cards or talk about it openly. In fact, those who grieve their child killed by abortion are often made to feel silly for feeling sad. After all, they are told by society that they exercised a choice that solved a problem. Why grieve over that?

Such questions, of course, reveal a complete blindness to the fact that killing one's child *hurts*, and leaves a wound that Mom does not ever forget.

These women are tired of having pro-choice advocates pretend to speak for them. They want to tell the world, in their own words, that what is too easily celebrated as a "choice" and a "right" is in fact a painful burden.

Not every post-abortive woman has found enough healing to be able to participate in these public rallies or hold these signs. But the participants in *Silent No More* pray that their presence will assist their sisters on the road to healing, and give them some measure of comfort to know that their grief is no longer forbidden.

Part IV
The Babies

Abortion: The Body Forgotten

THE woman who was about to have her abortion one Thursday morning was talking to me in sad tones about her child. "I know I am carrying a child," she said, "and I know God has given me this child. But I am not ready now. So, I am giving the child back to God."

That morning was not the only time I heard those same words from a mother about to abort her child. In fact, I have heard it time and time again, as have other pro-life counselors.

"I am giving the child back to God." One of the problems with this statement is that it ignores the fact that the child is about to be destroyed. Yes, we believe in the immortality of the soul and in the reality of the life of the world to come. But the child is not a soul. The child is a human person consisting of a soul and a body. The act of abortion destroys that human person. It crushes the body.

To dismiss this reality and say, "I'm giving the child back to God" feeds into a way of thinking that is pretty common these days, namely, that the body really doesn't matter. In reality, however, it matters as much as the soul, because the body is just as much an aspect of the human person as the soul is. What happens to your body happens to *you*. To take care of your body is to take care of *yourself*; to destroy your body is to destroy *you*. Some say, "I can do what I want with my body." But look carefully at that statement. The "I" and the "body" are separated. The body becomes *something I use, something with which I do something else.* But my body is not a thing I have and use, like my pen or my car. My body is me!

The Church has always rejected the idea that a human being is a spirit who simply uses the body as a tool. If only the soul matters, then people can say things like, "If we love each other, why is sex wrong? As long as we have the right intention, our physical actions are OK!" In other words, the *intention* (an action of the soul!) is all that counts.

Follow this thinking further, and you end up saying, "If my body doesn't work well anymore, and is more trouble than it is worth, I have the right to be free from that burden! I have the right to die!" Again, the act of killing the suffering person is not seen for what it is, namely, destroying the person, but rather simply as an escape of the *real person* from his or her body!

To be free from the culture of death demands a new appreciation of the body. When we say we are made in God's image, we mean our bodies, too! Respect for life means respect for *bodily* life, a body nourished by the very Body of Christ, and destined, like His, to rise from the dead!

"I Would Bury Him . . ." (Tobit 1:18)

A QUESTION that haunts many people about abortion is "What do they do with the bodies?" Stories continue to surface of people finding bodies of aborted babies in the trash, and many will recall the incident in the early 80s of the 16,500 bodies discovered in a large receptacle in Southern California. Meanwhile, it is well known that abortionist George Tiller has a crematorium in his facility in Wichita. Luhra Tivis, who once worked there, says in her testimony, "I could smell the babies burning."

In an abortion debate held in Italy some years ago, a pro-abortion leader challenged a Catholic opponent, "If you really believe these fetuses are persons, why doesn't the Church bury them?"

Glad you asked.

The fact is, we do. And there is a growing movement to make the proper and dignified burial of aborted children more widely known and practiced. I recently had a priest visit me in my office at the Pontifical Council for the Family in Rome. He has an association in Italy which works to lawfully obtain fetuses that have been aborted or miscarried and give them ceremonial burial.

This practice is, of course, one of the corporal works of mercy, *to bury the dead*. The Book of Tobit contains the touching story of how Tobit would bury the dead at great sacrifice to himself. "If I saw one of my people who had died and been thrown outside the walls of Nineveh, I would bury him. I also buried anyone whom Sennacherib slew. . . . In his rage he killed many Israelites, but I used to take their bodies by stealth and bury them" (Tob 1:18).

We understand the importance of treating the body with respect when we reflect that the human person is not merely a soul that "uses" a body, but is just as much a body as a soul. The body is not a thing I use. The body is personal, an aspect of "me." The body of the Christian, furthermore, becomes a temple of the Holy Spirit (1 Cor 6:19) and, through union with the very flesh of Christ in the Eucharist, is destined for Resurrection (Jn 6:54; see also Rom 8:11).

In the case of the 16,500 bodies found . . . the pro-abortion crowd fought hard for three years to prevent their proper burial. That would concede too much, they said. That would be too strong a sign that they are human.

If respect for the human body grows, tolerance of abortion will decrease. Let us pray for the success of movements of mercy like that in Italy which buries the babies that others rejected. Let us continue, in discussion and action, to raise the critical issue of *what happens to the bodies.* Let us continue, as the People of God, to proclaim that in every precious child's body, we have another manifestation of the glory of God Himself.

Unborn Pain

"IT is therefore declared to be the policy of the United States that the slaughtering of livestock and the handling of livestock in connection with slaughter shall be carried out only by humane methods."

Those words come from the "Humane Methods of Slaughter Act," a law that expresses our concern for the pain experienced by animals, but that more fundamentally expresses a dimension of our own humanity. In Australia, the national Health and Medical Research Council requires painkillers to be used *on the fetuses* of animals!

So what about *human* fetuses?

On April 6, 2004, the following testimony was given in U.S. District Court (District of Nebraska) by Dr. Kanwaljeet Anand before Judge Richard G. Kopf in the case of *Leroy Carhart, M.D., et. al. v. Ashcroft:*

Q. So, Doctor, do you have an opinion as to whether the partial-birth abortion procedure causes pain to the fetus?

A. If the fetus is beyond 20 weeks of gestation, I would assume that there will be pain caused to the fetus. And I believe it will be severe and excruciating pain caused to the fetus.

Q. What do you mean by severe and excruciating pain?

A. You see, the threshold for pain is very low. The fetus is very likely extremely sensitive to pain during the gestation of 20 to 30 weeks. And so the procedures associated with the partial-birth abortion that I just described would be likely to cause severe pain, right from the time the fetus is being manipulated and being handled to the time that the incision is made, and the brain or the contents, intracranial contents, are sucked out.

In 1994, an article in the prestigious British medical journal, *The Lancet,* revealed hormonal stress reactions in the fetus. The article concluded with the recommendation that painkillers be used when surgery is done on the fetus. The authors wrote, "This applies not just to diagnostic and therapeutic procedures on the fetus, but possibly also to termination of pregnancy, especially by surgical techniques involving dismemberment." In 1991, scientific advisors to the Federal Medical Council in Germany had made a similar recommendation.

In August 2001, Great Britain's Medical Research Council concluded that pain perception may be as early as 20 weeks; other studies place it as early as 10 weeks.

It should be noted that each year in the United States alone, over 18,000 abortions take place at 21 or more weeks of pregnancy.

The Unborn Child Pain Awareness Act has now been introduced in Congress, to inform women having abortions at 20 weeks or more that their baby may feel pain. The legislation deserves our support. It would require that the mother be given the option to provide painkillers to her baby. This is not to justify abortion, but will certainly make many think twice about it.

Many abortion supporters will, of course, continue to deny reality. As Bertrand Russell wrote, "A fisherman once told me that fish have neither sense nor sensation, but how he knew this, he could not tell me."

Fetal Memory

WHEN faced with the competing claims of two women about who was the mother of a newborn baby, King Solomon found the truth by threatening to have the baby cut in half.

Had he known of the research of behavioral scientist Stephen Evans, however, he might have asked for each mother's favorite music to be played.

Stephen Evans has conducted research that shows how babies who hear particular pieces of music while in their mother's womb will remember and recognize that music after birth. Mr. Evans took unique musical selections and had mothers play them for their baby *in utero* for 16 minutes a day, for seven days in a row, during the 20th week of pregnancy. Then he took the music back so it would not be heard by the child until after birth.

After birth, he played the music for the child and likewise for a control group of children who had never heard the music. The results surpassed his highest expectations. While any baby will normally calm down upon hearing music, the babies who had heard the music at 20 weeks were dramatically more calm when they heard it than were the babies who were hearing it for the first time.

Similar findings in various areas of fetal learning, fetal memory, and fetal psychology have been reported in recent years. There are even international associations dedicated to the psychology of the baby in the womb.

A natural question that arises, of course, is whether those who consider themselves to be "pro-choice" have heard of these findings, and whether it impacts their view of abortion.

Most people are affected by this research. Simply put, the "fetus" is revealed to be more and more like the newborn, and permitting the fetus to be killed begins to look about as unattractive as permitting the newborn to be killed.

But some will try to maintain that research about the fetus has nothing to do with abortion. *Psychology Today* featured a story in September 1998 about fetal psychology. A sidebar to that story asked, "What's the Impact on Abortion?" "I don't think that fetal research informs the issue at all," responded psychologist Janet DiPietro. Another psychologist, Heidelise Als, said, "If you believe that life begins at conception, then you don't need the proof of fetal behavior . . . Your circumstances and personal beliefs have much more impact on the decision."

That kind of side-stepping is pretty unpersuasive. When we separate "beliefs" from any kind of supporting evidence, we end up in a "fideism" that Christianity has always rejected. Christian faith, even about things that cannot be demonstrated by science, is always connected to rational motives for believing.

Moreover, victims of past abuse—like African Americans burdened by slavery and segregation, or children burdened by child labor—have had their rights recognized based on mounting evidence of the harm being inflicted on them.

Whether some want to deny it or not, the same is happening now for the unborn.

And You Thought Partial Birth
Abortion Was Bad . . .

I WILL never forget the day when I came across Dr. Martin Haskell's medical paper "Dilation and Extraction for Late Second Trimester Abortion," presented at the National Abortion Federation Risk Management Seminar, September 13, 1992. It describes what has come to be known as "partial-birth abortion." *"[T]he surgeon then forces the scissors into the base of the skull or into the* foramen magnum. *Having safely entered the skull, he spreads the scissors to enlarge the opening. The surgeon removes the scissors and introduces a suction catheter into this hole and evacuates the skull contents."*

Prior to the days when partial-birth abortion was in the news or debated in the halls of Congress, I began taking this paper to parishes across the country and speaking and preaching about it. Others had likewise discovered the paper and were doing the same thing. There are still too many people who don't know about it, but certainly a great awareness has been generated, and in fact President George Bush signed the ban on partial-birth abortion on November 5, 2003. I spoke to Dr. Haskell more than once about the procedure. "There does not seem to be any medical reason for the procedure," he told me. A woman obtains it, he explained, because she wants an abortion.

I have on my desk the words of another doctor, Warren M. Hern, in his book *Abortion Practice*. It is a medical textbook on how to do abortions, and in it he describes another procedure which must also be made better known to the public. The procedure is called Dilatation and Evacuation (D&E), and differs from "partial birth abortion" in that the child is not partially delivered, but rather dismembered within the womb. He describes the procedure at various stages of pregnancy, starting at 13 weeks. I quote here from the section "21 to 24 Weeks Fetal Age":

"The procedure changes significantly at 21 weeks because the fetal tissues become much more cohesive and difficult to dismember. This problem is accentuated by the fact that the fetal pelvis may be as much as 5cm in width. The *calvaria* [head] is no longer the principal problem; it can be collapsed. Other structures, such as the pelvis, present more difficulty. . . . A long curved Mayo scissors may be necessary to decapitate and dismember the fetus . . ."(p.154).

He speaks of the crushing of the head in these terms: "As the *calvaria* is grasped, a sensation that it is collapsing is almost always accompanied by the extrusion of white cerebral material from the external os" (p.142).

Dr. Hern also admits that a "disadvantage of the D&E procedure is that it is objectionable to physicians and their assistants." But, he goes on, "It is of utmost importance to keep in mind the advantages that the procedure offers for patients. . . ." (p.134)

Some people are tired of the abortion controversy in our nation. Frankly, I often wonder whether it has even begun. Maybe when it becomes more widely known that things like what I quoted above are legally occurring every day—maybe then the debate can begin.

Images

"I HAVE been a pro-choice believer my entire life until someone shared your web-site with me. I was first shocked then sickened by what I saw. God, how could I have been so misguided my entire life? I actually believed it was not a baby. I actually believed a first trimester abortion was fine. Boy did you open my eyes. I believe that God worked with me today to show me the right way. I have often wondered if I was wrong but always dismissed those thoughts until I saw these photographs."

I have always been convinced that showing people pictures of aborted babies is a powerful way to convince them that abortion is wrong. Because of this, I recently posted several galleries of such images on my website, at www.priestsforlife.org/images. Now despite the fact that the Priests for Life website has thousands of pages of print, and hundreds of hours of audio files, nothing on that site has changed more minds about abortion than the pictures. No pages are visited more frequently, and we keep getting emails like the one above, and like these:

"I'm 25, white . . . from a middle class family in NY. Before seeing this site I was 100% pro choice . . . However after seeing these photos, I can honestly say I have changed my opinion."

"Your website has completely changed my views. I, personally, did not believe in abortions, but I felt it should be left up to the woman. Now I have realized that the 'glob of tissue' the abortion clinics often talk about is truly a human being. I will pass information about this website along to everyone I know. Thank you so much. You have saved more unborn babies' lives than you'll ever know."

"Up until now I've been indecisive on the subject of abortion, unable to decide if a fetus could be considered a person, a living thing. After seeing these images I am now against this horrific procedure."

The images also have an impact on those who are already pro-life, as the following email indicates:

"Today, I saw your website with the photos of the aborted babies and wept. I have always been anti-abortion and have voted against any candidate whose party or platform supports abortion. However, like many of the uninformed masses, abortion was something abstract, impersonal yet immoral. Your web site has changed my view of abortion forever."

There is no "magic answer" to end abortion in our nation, and I interact every day with many pro-life groups and leaders to support many different strategies. But it is a big mistake to think that the pictures "don't work" or "everyone knows" what abortion is. The more you use the photos, the more you learn that the opposite is true. They make a hidden injustice visible.

You are free to download the images and their medical authentication at www.priestsforlife.org/images. If people you know are unsure about abortion, send them to that web page. They will never be the same.

Part V

The Celebrations

A Special Anniversary

MARCH 25, 2005 marked the tenth anniversary of Pope John Paul II's encyclical *The Gospel of Life (Evangelium Vitae)*. This is not just another document. It is literally a celebration. It celebrates Christ, who is personally the Gospel and the Life. It celebrates humanity, love, and true freedom.

The Church knows how to celebrate; the world has forgotten. The Church knows how to receive and give life and love. In fact, the very meaning of life is to give *and* receive love (#81). But the world has become too preoccupied with usefulness, efficiency, and productivity (#22). The world is too busy with its frantic flight from all suffering and death (#64, #66-67). It flees these because it has forgotten what they mean. It sees them only as things to be avoided and controlled. Ironically, such forgetfulness envelops the world even more in the very things it tries to escape. And in the midst of its slavery to death, the world shouts about freedom, all the while fearing it will be shackled by the one who brings true freedom, namely, Christ.

The world needs "good news," that is, *"Evangelium."* The document begins, "The Gospel *(Evangelium)* of life is at the heart of Jesus' message. Lovingly received day after day by the Church, it is to be preached with dauntless fidelity as good news to the people of every age and culture" (#1).

Life is joyful, so it is to be proclaimed (#80-82), celebrated (#83-86) and served (#87-89). The message of life is not optional, or added on to the Gospel, but is at the heart of the Gospel. The Gospel of Life is simply the Gospel of

Christ, for He is Life (see #29). The Church is inescapably pro-life (#28) precisely because she is feminine. The Church is the Bride of Christ and Mother of believers—and, in fact, of all humanity (#3).

The earth today is covered with innocent blood, which cries out from the ground to the God who made it (see #7-9, Gen 4:2-16). But thanks be to God, there is another Blood that cries out to heaven more eloquently (see #25, Heb 12:22, 24). The cry of the Blood of Christ brings mercy to those who shed the blood of their brothers and sisters. The shed Blood of Christ teaches the meaning of love, which is to sacrifice oneself for the good of the other person. It reverses the dynamic of the culture of death, which sacrifices the other person for the good of oneself. The Blood of Christ, one drop of which can purify a billion worlds, gives us strength to carry out the "great campaign on behalf of life" which is called for by this encyclical (#95). The pro-life movement itself, in fact, is a sign of hope and victory (#26). The encyclical looks to the day when "death will be no more" (Rev 21:4 see #105). That time is coming, and that promise is, in a nutshell, the Gospel of Life.

No Room in the Inn

"SHE wrapped him in swaddling cloths and laid him in a manger, because there was no room for them in the inn" (Lk 2:7).

The fact that there was no room for Jesus, Mary, and Joseph in the inn at Bethlehem on the first Christmas should make us wonder, because the birth of Christ was foreseen and planned by God from all eternity. Hundreds of years before it happened, the prophets announced he would be born of a virgin (Is 7:14) and that Bethlehem would be his birthplace (Mic 5:2). Many other details of his life and death were also foretold. Did God, then, forget to make room for his only Son? How is it possible that there was no room, when the child born at Christmas owns the inn, and Bethlehem, and the world, and every inch of room in the whole universe?

Obviously, God did this on purpose. There was no room in the inn, because this demonstrates that the world has rejected God. The world makes no room for the God who created it. There was no room in the inn because God wanted to show that His Son comes as a Savior, to reconcile a world that is at enmity with God. Being turned away from the inn foreshadows the fact that the Savior himself will be rejected, despised, and ultimately crucified, and that all this was part of God's plan from all eternity. Ultimately, the lack of room in the inn symbolizes the lack of room we make for Him in our hearts. When our hearts are filled with all kinds of other desires than God, we gradually crowd Him out altogether.

No room at the inn also means that we fail to make room for our brothers and sisters. The first great commandment is to love God, and the second is like it: Love your neighbor. Christ willed to be left out, because He is always in solidarity with those who are left out, shut out, and crowded out. That is the position of the unborn children today. They are crowded out of the busy schedules of so many people doing so many good and important things, but who don't have a finger to lift to protect the lives of these children from abortion. They are crowded out of legislative agendas, preaching schedules, career plans, and volunteer activities. There's just too much going on already; there's no room in the inn.

Christ comes at Christmas to change all that. Today, He does not seek an inn; He seeks room in our own hearts and lives. And He asks that as we welcome Him, we welcome everyone whom He welcomes, including the children most defenseless and forgotten. We welcome the Divine Child, and in doing so, we welcome every child. As we celebrate Christmas, we sing in "O Holy Night" the words, "Chains shall He break, for the slave is our brother, and in His name all oppression shall cease." Amen! Let oppression cease and let Christmas come for the unborn!

Choice on Earth

SEVERAL years ago during the holiday season a lot of attention was on a Christmas card produced by the nation's largest single abortion provider, Planned Parenthood.

The message of the card? "Choice on Earth."

Planned Parenthood advertises the card as containing "an inclusive seasonal message." Inclusive for everyone, of course, except the unborn child, who is destroyed by the so-called "choice" that Planned Parenthood defends.

But, of course, Planned Parenthood is not ashamed. In fact, when their card was called anti-Christian, they responded by adding a "Choice on Earth" T-shirt to their line of products.

Added to this, some who call themselves ministers of the Gospel preached their seasonal message by claiming that Jesus would not have been against the "choice" of a woman regarding whether or not to continue her pregnancy. You may be aware that there is a "Clergy for Choice Network" operated by the "Religious Coalition for Reproductive Choice."

My comment on all of this is that it should not surprise us in the least. The essence of the abortion mentality is *not* to deny that the unborn child is a child. Rather, it is that *we take the place of God*. It is the idea that *what I choose is right*, not because the thing I choose is *good*, but rather because I *choose*. Choice is more important than life, and my choice takes the place of God Himself. Hence, clergy preach "choice" and the message of Christ becomes "choice on earth."

Ultimately, human beings have to feel like they are in line with God. Therefore, if they do not change their lives to conform to God's will, they will change their very concept of God to conform to their own will. That's what the "Choice on Earth" cards demonstrate.

The notion that Christ does not have a problem with the choice to destroy an unborn child turns the Gospel inside out. By giving His life for us, Christ teaches the essence of love: *I sacrifice myself for the good of the other person.* Abortion teaches exactly the opposite message: *I sacrifice the other person for the good of myself.*

Jesus, furthermore, broke down false barriers that placed people in "higher" and "lower" social and spiritual categories. He ate with tax collectors and sinners when the common wisdom was to avoid them. He sought out the lepers when the custom was to stay away from them. He called the children to come to Him, when the apostles thought that the right thing to do was to chase them away. He gave the Samaritan woman the gift of salvation, breaking through barriers that put both Samaritans and women on a lower level.

Does it make sense, then, that the Lord permits the false barrier between the born and the unborn, and does not mind the discrimination by which the unborn are considered disposable *non-persons*?

God is a God of *justice*—in other words, He saves the helpless. And He expects us to do no less. *That's* peace on earth.

A Pro-life Lent

"REPENT and believe the Good News!"

The urgent call to repent marks the Lenten season, just as it marks the preaching ministry of St. John the Baptist (Mt 3:2), of the Lord Jesus (Mt 4:17), and of Peter and the Apostles (Acts 2:37-38). It is a call to make a conscious and free choice to turn away from sin, which leads to death, and embrace the Gospel, which leads to life. It is, in fact, the full flowering of the call Moses issued in Deuteronomy 30:19, "I have set before you life and death . . . Choose life!"

One of my favorite Lenten Gospel passages is that of the man born blind (John 9). We see here the drama of the will to accept or reject the call of Christ. The man born blind receives his physical sight early in the story, but the rest of the drama traces the birth of his spiritual sight. At first, he calls Jesus a man (v. 11); then a prophet (v. 17); then one who is "from God" (v. 33), and finally, "Lord" (v. 38). He comes to see who Jesus is, because he has a willingness to believe. "Who is he, sir, that I may believe in him?" (v. 36).

This attitude of willingness stands in stark contrast to the stubbornness and bad will of the Pharisees. Though confronted with the same evidence of the physical healing, they try to explain away that evidence through their interrogations of the man and his parents, and then by portraying Jesus as a sinner, and finally by literally throwing the evidence out the door by ejecting the healed man from their midst (see v. 34).

The drama is repeated every day as our society struggles with the "Culture of Death," which shows itself fundamentally in the ongoing tragedy of abortion. The evidence is the same for all to see, made clearer than ever by genetics and fetology, that abortion kills a human being. Some receive that evidence and, with a willing heart, choose life. Others show the stubbornness of the Pharisees and cling to their own ideology. For me the most stark example of this was the day a group of pro-life people conducted a wake for an aborted baby in front of an abortion facility. The baby, the size of a hand, was visible in a small white casket. Some pro-abortion demonstrators looked at the child, and a pro-lifer challenged them, "Look at the evidence right before your eyes. This is a baby!" Believe it or not, the person's response was "That's your opinion!!"

Not to know the child in the womb is not a sin. But the refusal to know is. Jesus declares to the Pharisees at the end of the drama of John 9, "If you were blind, there would be no sin in that, but 'We see,' you say, and your sin remains" (v. 41).

"Repent and believe the Good News!" What good news? The good news, in the words of *The Gospel of Life,* that "life is always a good . . . a manifestation of God in the world, a sign of His presence, a trace of His glory" (#34). This Lent, let us choose life again!

A Kingdom Conquered

"*D*UX *vitae mortuus, regnat vivus*"—"Life's Captain, who died, now lives and reigns."

These words come from the ancient Easter Sequence, the *Victimae Paschali*, which is proclaimed before the Gospel on Easter Sunday Masses. The message is clear: Easter is not simply about someone rising from the dead; it is about the conquering of a Kingdom. Life's Captain not only lives; He also reigns. He has a kingdom, and it is the Kingdom of Life. Jesus is explicit about this when speaking to the apostles after His Resurrection. "All authority in heaven and on earth has been given to me" (Mt 28:18).

Death is not merely a single event. It, too, is a kingdom, to which some choose to belong. "But through the devil's envy, death entered the world, and those who belong to him experience it" (Wis 2:24). Yet God "has rescued us from the power of darkness and brought us into the kingdom of his beloved Son" (Col 1:13; see also Heb 2:14-15). Christ, by rising, has not only overcome His own death; He has overcome ours! He has overturned the entire kingdom of death.

The effects of that defeated kingdom do, indeed, endure, even as the Kingdom of God makes progress in growth through the phases of human history. Pope John Paul II has pointed out the existence of "a kind of 'conspiracy against life,' " a "war of the powerful against the weak" in our day (see *The Gospel of Life* (EV), n. 12).

Yet in working to overcome this culture of death, marked most tragically by abortion, we are not simply working "for victory." We, rather, are working "from victory!" Victory is our starting point. Christ is Risen! This concrete, historical event, in all its truth and significance, contains the objective defeat of the culture of death. The Victory of Life, furthermore, is present in every Mass, where we proclaim, "Dying you destroyed our death; Rising you restored our life!"

Easter gives us our identity as "the people of life" (EV n.79). Baptized into Christ's victory over death, we are also sent to proclaim, celebrate, and serve that victory (see EV 78-101). At Easter Mass, we renew the vows of our baptism, one of which is that we "reject Satan and all his works." Chief among those works is death. Yet the Son of God has destroyed death, and that means that we who follow Him likewise are called to stand against it.

Many who sincerely believe may not realize the full implications of that belief. To believe in and celebrate the Resurrection necessarily immerses us in and commits us to the conflict against evils such as abortion and euthanasia. We are not free to ignore the battle or entrust it to someone else. It belongs to our very identity to fight it. It belongs to the very identity of the priest, furthermore, to preach it.

And it belongs to our identity to do all this with the utmost serenity, confidence, and joy. Christ is truly Risen and is with us! Let us rejoice and be glad!

Annunciation

WHEN I served at the Vatican's Pontifical Council for the Family, a frequent theme that came up in meetings with pro-life leaders from around the world was the special importance of the Feast of the Annunciation for the pro-life movement, and a desire to see that Feastday given even more prominence in the celebrations of the Church.

The significance exists on several levels.

The Annunciation, when the Virgin Mary is told that she has been chosen to be the Mother of the Savior, constitutes the moment when "the Word became Flesh." The eternal Son of God began existing as a human being not at His birth at Bethlehem, but within the womb of Mary.

God was once an unborn child. Every unborn child, therefore, is in some fashion united with God. As the Second Vatican Council asserted, "By his incarnation the Son of God has united himself in some fashion with every human being" (Pastoral Constitution on the Church in the Modern World, *Gaudium et Spes*, 22).

In the writings of the Fathers of the Church, we encounter reflections on the theme that Christ redeemed us by assuming all the different aspects of our life on earth, including our childhood, our life of work, our family life, our sufferings, and our death. In an age when, as Pope John Paul II said, "it is possible to speak in a certain sense of a war of the powerful against the weak" (*The Gospel of Life*, 12), we should also reflect on the fact that the Son of God shared in our life in the womb.

Would it long be possible for believers, who meditate on the unborn child who was God, to fail to see that unborn children are made in God's image? Would it be likely that those who ponder that our Almighty Protector was a baby in the womb will fail to see that babies in the womb deserve protection? Would it happen that Christians, who acknowledge that their Lord and Brother was an embryo and fetus, will fail to see that every embryo and fetus is a brother and sister in the Lord?

Yet the marvels revealed by the Annunciation do not stop there. There is also the mystery of Mary's freedom, her *"Fiat"*—"Let it be done to me according to your word" (Lk 1:38). This is freedom of choice which serves the truth, as opposed to "pro-choice" which claims to create its own truth. This is choice at the service of life, rather than the perverted choice to take life. This is the moment when Mary gave her body to the One who would bring life to the world by saying "This is My Body," forever undoing the sin of those who justify abortion by saying, "This is my body!"

Yes, let us celebrate the Annunciation with greater solemnity than ever before. Let us join the spirit of those nations which have declared March 25 a day of the unborn child. Let us recommit ourselves to love and serve the weakest among us!

Graduation Day

MY high school graduation is one of my most pleasant memories. It was a bright, sunny day in 1976. We were the "Bicentennial" class. I was privileged to address my fellow graduates, and I had been advised not to speak of any "controversial" issues. I didn't. Though it was a public school, I spoke of God, faith, and service in my remarks.

But that was also the year I became more aware of the "controversial issue" that had exploded just three years earlier with the Roe vs. Wade abortion decision. If I knew then what I know now, my speech would have been about abortion, no matter what "advice" anyone may have given me.

Several years ago, I came across a story of a graduating class which dedicated its yearbook to all the students who would have been graduating that year had they not been killed—by abortion. How fitting a tribute that is. Other graduating classes have paid tribute to their abortion victims by a moment of prayer at the Baccalaureate mass or at the graduation ceremony.

And why not? Suppose that a tragedy took the lives of some of the graduating class just days or weeks before graduation. Would there not be a mention or a tribute at the ceremony? Why, then, should the victims who died longer ago be forgotten? It is not, after all, the timing of the death that matters, but the value of the life.

In 2002, the Alan Guttmacher Institute, a research division of Planned Parenthood, reported 1.29 million abortions. If you find another single act or disaster that claims that many lives in our country alone in a single year, please let me know about it.

At graduation time I happily recall my own, and pray for all graduates at all different grade levels. It is my fervent hope that students everywhere will take the initiative to remember aborted classmates.

Some, of course, will object to inserting such a "negative" theme into a happy day.

Yes, life is tough, isn't it? . . . It's all mixed up with happiness and sadness, joy and tragedy. Are significant moments in our lives supposed to be insulated from all awareness of injustice? Are we to rejoice with those who rejoice, but not weep with those who weep?

To be willing to acknowledge tragedy among those of us already born, but to be unwilling to do so when the very tragedy is that some never had the chance to be born, is another sign of the deep-rooted prejudice against the unborn in our society. But a new generation of young people who have survived that prejudice are now taking their places and preparing to be the future leaders. That gives us hope. Isn't that what Graduation Day is all about?

The Fourth of July

THE Fourth of July is one of my favorite days.

Living across the street from a public high school field from which the town fireworks display was launched each year made it extra special, as did the presence of many relatives and friends who would come to our house to celebrate the day (as well as my father's and brother's birthdays).

As a priest, furthermore, I enjoy offering the prayers of the liturgy for Independence Day. The Preface is particularly inspiring. It reads in part,

"[Christ] spoke to men a message of peace and taught us to live as brothers. His message took form in the vision of our fathers as they fashioned a nation where men might live as one. This message lives on in our midst as a task for men today and a promise for tomorrow. We thank you, Father, for your blessings in the past and for all that, with your help, we must yet achieve" (*Sacramentary*, Preface for Independence Day I, P82).

The blessings we give thanks for on the Fourth of July are many. I have come to realize that more than ever as I have had occasion in the last few years to speak on almost every continent. We give thanks not only for material possessions and for freedom, but for the vision behind them. The vision is that "men might live as one"; the vision is that all will be welcomed, as the Statue of Liberty symbolizes; the vision is that "all are created equal"; the vision is "liberty and justice for all."

It is a vision that we do not merely look back on, thanking God that our Founding Fathers had it. It is, rather, a vision which is "a task for today and a promise for tomorrow."

This is why the pro-life movement is so American. It is a movement striving to achieve welcome for those of whom *Roe vs. Wade* spoke when it said, "The word 'person,' as used in the Fourteenth Amendment, does not include the unborn" (*Roe vs. Wade,* at 158). *Roe* excluded; the pro-life movement includes. *Roe* made the circle of persons in America smaller; the pro-life movement seeks to expand it.

One Fourth of July, some friends of mine and I held a banner in front of my house as all the people gathered across the street for the fireworks. It said, "Pray to end Abortion." One man, expressing agreement with the message, questioned whether it was the right setting to deliver it. "Of course it is," I explained. "This is the day we celebrate a nation in which all are supposed to be considered equal. What better way to celebrate our freedom than to work to extend it to others?"

As I celebrate Mass on the Fourth of July, I pray that our celebrations will renew our determination to work for justice and freedom for all unborn Americans.

Part VI

The Abortionists

"Crummy Medicine"

THE practice of abortion today is a far cry from what *Roe vs. Wade* had in mind, and abortionists know it.

Dr. Warren Hern, who wrote a medical textbook on how to do abortions, said the following at the 18th Annual meeting of the National Abortion Federation:

"I have to say this: There's a lot of crummy medicine being practiced out there in providing abortion services, and I think that some of the stuff I see coming across my desk is very upsetting . . . We have to do this right or we shouldn't do it."

That's almost as reassuring as the words of Dr. Edward Allred, owner of a chain of abortion facilities performing some 60,000 abortions per year:

"Very commonly we hear patients say they feel like they're on an assembly line. We tell them they're right. It is an assembly line . . . We're trying to be as cost-effective as possible, and speed is important . . . We try to use the physician for his technical skills and reduce the one-on-one relationship with the patient. We usually see the patient for the first time on the operating table and then not again . . . " ("Doctor's Abortion Business is Lucrative," San Diego Union, Oct. 12, 1980: B1).

What many don't realize is that *Roe vs. Wade* didn't mean to leave the abortion decision only up to the woman. It decided, rather, that the "right to privacy" was broad enough to encompass abortion, which was to be practiced only after appropriate and sufficient consultation with a responsible physician. The Court said,

" . . . Appellants . . . argue that the woman's right is absolute and that she is entitled to terminate her pregnancy at whatever time, in whatever way, and for whatever reason she alone chooses. With this we do not agree . . . The Court's decisions recognizing a right of privacy also acknowledge that some state regulation in areas protected by that right is appropriate. As noted above, a state may properly assert important interests in safeguarding health, in maintaining medical standards, and in protecting potential life . . . The privacy right involved, therefore, cannot be said to be absolute."

In reference to malpractice, *Roe* also said, "If an individual practitioner abuses the privilege of exercising proper medical judgment, the usual remedies, judicial and intra-professional, are available" (*Roe* at 166).

Medical professionals have also acknowledged these issues:

"It is recognized that although an abortion may be requested by a patient or recommended by a physician, the final decision as to performing the abortion must be left to the medical judgment of the pregnant woman's attending physician, in consultation with the patient" (American College of Obstetricians and Gynecologists: Committee on Professional Standards, Standard for Obstetric-Gynecological Services, 1981).

Abortion is legal, but malpractice is not. My hunch is that if we crack down on the malpractice, abortion itself will decline. After all, you can't practice vice virtuously. When we speak of these things, the abortion industry accuses us of "harassment." That's a strange way to label efforts to protect women. Maybe it's time for supporters of *Roe vs. Wade* to reread it.

Easy Prey

WHAT place of business in America can a woman walk into and be at the highest risk of becoming a victim of rape?

The answer is a legal abortion clinic.

More and more stories are coming to light of various types of mistreatment of clients in abortion clinics— deceptive practices, manipulative pressures, unsanitary instruments, falsifying of records, people posing as doctors without having spent a day in medical school, injuries, and deaths. In some cases this leads to new bills in state legislatures seeking to regulate abortion clinics; in other cases it leads to the closing of the clinics and the jailing of the abortionist.

Certainly one of the most troubling elements of this picture is the prevalence of sexual assault in abortion clinics. It is not uncommon. (One of the sources that documents this information is the book *Lime 5* by Mark Crutcher.)

Why is this happening? Several factors account for it.

First of all, when a woman is in an abortion facility, she's in a place where she doesn't want others to know she is. Usually she has hidden the fact that she is sexually active, now needs to hide the fact that she's pregnant, and will later hide the fact that she had an abortion. If, therefore, she is sexually assaulted by the abortionist, whom does she tell?

A good analogy provided by the author of *Lime 5* is of a married man going to a prostitute, and in the course of his visit a man jumps out from hiding, beats him, and steals his wallet. Now what does he do, tell his wife that his wallet was stolen during a visit to a prostitute?

Added to the shame of saying anything about it is the fact that the abortion client is already naked and usually anesthetized.

Another factor contributing to the occurrence of sexual assault in abortion clinics is the moral degeneracy of the abortionists. The documented evidence we have from cases all over the country shows a pattern of immoral behavior connected with the practice of abortion—lying, theft, substance abuse, infidelity, and violence, including sexual violence.

A Bureau of Justice study from 2002 estimated that only 36% of rapes were reported to police between 1992-2000. If that is the case in general, the underreporting of rape in abortion clinics is much higher, based on the considerations outlined above. Usually those who report these instances are non-abortion victims of the abortionist's acts.

The cases in which abortionists have been convicted of sexual assault, furthermore, reveal that the attacks are not about power, but about punishment. It seems as though the resentment which abortion providers feel because they have to do something that everyone considers "dirty work" is taken out on the woman who seeks the abortion. (See the psychological studies of Dr. Philip Ney on why people become abortionists.)

Does anybody hear anything from "pro-woman, pro-choice" groups—or candidates—in protest of this sexual assault?

The Neglected Side of *Roe vs. Wade*

YOU don't hear much about it, but the fact is that *Roe vs. Wade* did not simply give a woman the right to an abortion. It placed on the physician the responsibility to insure the safety of the woman who gets an abortion.

And that's where the supporters of *Roe vs. Wade* fail to implement *Roe vs. Wade*.

Abortion remains the most unregulated surgical industry in the nation. Some 93% of abortions are not performed in hospitals, but rather in "clinics" which most states exempt from regulation. In fact, in the vast majority of states, veterinary clinics are more regulated than abortion clinics.

Just look at the laws that are or are not on the books. First of all, an abortionist does not have to have a specialty in OB-GYN. Rather, your abortionist may be a urologist, an allergist, or a plastic surgeon. What, furthermore, are the licensing requirements for the staff of abortion clinics? Usually, there are none. How about regulations regarding the presence of emergency medical equipment in the clinic, in case a complication should arise, or the laws governing how such an emergency should be handled? Let me know when you find such laws.

The question, of course, is why is abortion so unregulated? After all, if abortion is a legitimate medical procedure, should it not follow the same standards as other legitimate medical procedures?

The beginning of an answer may be found in the kinds of people who do abortions. Face it, one does not spend years of effort and tens of thousands of dollars to become a doctor in order to be known as an abortionist. Three decades of legalization have not taken the stigma out of abortion. "Fewer and fewer physicians wish to perform abortions" (Journal of Medical Ethics, Volume 22, 1996).

As a result, this area of "medical" practice remains as shady as it ever was, and attracts the losers and washouts of the medical community. I know many of those that used to perform abortions and no longer do. Some, in fact, posed as doctors without having spent a day in medical school. Others testify that they never sterilized the instruments. And stories of sexual abuse in abortion clinics abound. This, remember, is taking place in legal abortion clinics.

So what are we in the pro-life community asking? We are calling for a full investigation of what is going on in abortion clinics. Nobody knows how many abuses are happening, but the more you look, the more you find. Furthermore, we call for more states to exercise their constitutionally protected right to regulate abortion clinics. We are also calling on the "pro-choice" groups to be honest. Being in favor of women's rights and health should include action to insure that clinics protect women against the malpractice of unscrupulous abortionists. After all, if you care about the exploitation of women, you care about it no matter who is doing the exploiting.

Playing Defense

IF there's one thing the pro-abortion forces in this nation do not know how to do well, it's to play defense. They are so used to taking the first steps, framing the issues, and putting pro-life people and organizations on the defensive, that they hardly know what to do when the tables are turned.

Priests for Life has been turning those tables with full page ads in papers like the *Wall Street Journal* and *USA Today*. A recent series of these ads called on the abortion industry to account for the deaths and injuries of women in so-called "safe and legal" abortion clinics nationwide.

Consider what happens when an abortionist is killed. Not only is the presumption immediately and irresponsibly made that a "pro-life" person did this, but the abortion industry calls on the entire leadership of the pro-life movement to denounce this violence, separate themselves from it, and do everything possible to prevent it. Certainly we do denounce such violence, no matter who carries it out. But the dilemma that is created for us is that every time we denounce acts of violence at abortion facilities, we call attention to the fact that there has been violence at abortion facilities—and that's what the pro-abortion groups want the public to know.

Through our ads, we put the abortion industry in a similar dilemma. We know, through court cases, news stories, testimonies of former abortionists, and from the victims and their families, that women are abused, maimed, and killed in legal abortion clinics nationwide. Through the ads, we bring these facts out into the open. We take the initiative to expose this hidden tragedy.

What, then, are the pro-abortion forces to do? If they say anything, they have to distance themselves from the problem. "Oh, that doesn't happen in our clinic," many of them will say. "Our doctors have higher standards. We take more precautions than others; our facilities are safe and clean and regulated. No patient has died in our facilities."

Their very attempt to defend themselves calls attention to the fact that these tragedies have happened in at least some abortion clinics.

Their other option, of course, is that they can ignore the whole matter. But how, then, do they—claiming to champion women's rights and health—explain their silence in the face of women being abused, injured and killed?

Our ads are carefully documented in every detail. We offer a partial list of the names of women killed in abortion clinics as well as additional information about documented cases. (See our website at www.priestsforlife.org/brochures/maternaldeaths.html).

Nobody knows how many of these incidents occur, because they are carefully covered-up, including by falsification of medical records. This much is certain, however: the more one looks for these cases, the more one finds. And the more we find, the more we should proclaim it, and let the pro-aborts play defense for a change.

Coverup

THE abortion industry is in trouble, and it's time to capitalize on that trouble.

In every state, sexual activity with underage children is illegal. Moreover, if a health care worker suspects that a minor is being sexually abused, or is the victim of statutory rape, that worker is required by law to report the information to the authorities designated by the law. (Remember, statutory rape does not mean an "attack." It refers to the age of the parties.)

For many months, my friends and colleagues at Life Dynamics in Denton, Texas have been gathering more information about what an abortion clinic is likely to do if an underage girl who has been impregnated by an adult asks for an abortion. The fact that the abortion or birth control that the clinic sells is "legal" does not take away the clinic workers' responsibility to report. The requirement under the law, furthermore, for the health care worker is simply to report, not to investigate. In other words, the very fact that an underage girl is pregnant indicates that there may have been criminal activity or abuse. The health care worker does not have to investigate whether there was or not, but simply report that there might be.

What Life Dynamics did is described in their own words on their website, www.childpredators.com: "Life Dynamics conducted a covert investigation in which we called over 800 Planned Parenthood and National Abortion Federation facilities across the country. Our caller portrayed a 13-year-old girl who was pregnant by her 22-year-old boyfriend. Her story was that she wanted an abortion because she and her boyfriend did not want her parents to find out about the sexual relationship. In every call the ages of the girl and her boyfriend were made perfectly clear. It was also unmistakable that the motivation for the abortion was to conceal this illicit sexual activity from the girl's parents and the authorities. The results were appalling. Even though many of these clinic workers openly acknowledged to our caller that this situation was illegal and that they were required to report it to the state, the overwhelming majority readily agreed to conceal this illegal sexual activity. Some employees of these organizations even coached our caller on how to avoid detection, how to circumvent parental involvement laws and what to say or not say when she came to the clinic."

So what should be done next?

First of all, spread the word. People, especially those who are parents, have a right to know about the risks their children and grandchildren face in legal abortion clinics.

Secondly, legislation can be introduced to stop these clinics and their supporting organizations from receiving state and federal funding. After all, recipients of these funds are required to use the money only in accordance with all state and federal laws.

Thirdly, massive litigation should be launched against the abortion industry for engaging in this illegal activity.

Along with changing laws and hearts, we simply need to put abortionists out of business.

A Golden Opportunity

IT is widely known that many American schools allow Planned Parenthood and similar organizations on campus to discuss abortion, birth control, pregnancy, sexually transmitted diseases, and other issues related to the sexual activity of students. What is not so widely known is that Planned Parenthood gives away nothing for free. The students might not pay, but the taxpayers do, through Title X grants from the government. For Planned Parenthood to get its money, it needs to have access to the students—and the money comes even more through the birth control pills and STD treatments than it does through the abortions.

In other words, not only does Planned Parenthood bring its morally corrupted message to our children, grandchildren, nieces and nephews, but by doing so it gets from us the money it needs to continue to become more powerful and effective.

We now have a new way to stop this atrocity. You may have heard that new evidence has been collected demonstrating that the overwhelming majority of abortion facilities nationwide break the law by failing to report statutory rape. The clinics, in fact, have the duty to report any suspected sexual abuse of minors. When minors come to them for abortions, birth control, or pregnancy testing, that is all the reason they need to make a report.

Litigation is now being launched nationwide against these abortion clinics, and Planned Parenthood is a key defendant. In April 2005 in Indiana, Planned Parenthood fought to block the Attorney General from getting medical records of 14-year-old "patients," aka underage sexually active clients.

Here's where the schools come in. If your school district refers students to Planned Parenthood, and they in turn get into a lawsuit for failure to report, the school is exposed to legal trouble as well, because they can be guilty of negligent referral. If they get embroiled in a lawsuit, it is your tax money—whether you have a student in the school or not—that will have to pay for it.

Every school district in America has received a letter alerting them to this problem. Now, Priests for Life will coordinate an effort to have concerned taxpayers go to their school board meetings and ask questions like the following:

What is our School District doing to insure that the employees who provide referrals adhere to state laws requiring the reporting of sexual activity by underage children? How is our School District protecting itself legally against possible claims against it?

Right now the American people are taking seriously the issue of adults sexually abusing children and having it covered up by major institutions. Moreover, school boards are notoriously timid when it comes to knowingly exposing their districts to lawsuits. This effort can lead thousands of school districts to close their doors to Planned Parenthood!

We need people to go to their school board meetings. We will provide guidance, and specific questions that need to be raised. If you want to help, contact Priests for Life, School Protection Project, PO Box 141172, Staten Island, NY 10314, (718) 980-4400, ext. 297; email: schools@priestsforlife.org.

The Society of Centurions

I OFTEN say that I believe in the "dead-end rule." This is the rule that says that if you go down a dead-end street and don't see the sign that says it's a dead end, you will soon learn by personal experience that the road is a dead end.

For decades, the pro-life movement has been putting up dead-end signs along the road of abortion. Many choose to ignore those signs; others don't see them at all. But the fact is that individuals who become involved in abortion, and nations which embrace it as policy, eventually learn by painful experience that abortion is a dead end. Just try naming one societal ill which abortion has solved.

There is a special group of people who have come to the dead end and have resolutely begun walking the other way. They call themselves the Society of Centurions. They are former providers of abortion who have abandoned that practice and now embrace the sanctity of life. Their number includes physicians, nurses, paramedical personnel, technicians, receptionists, and security personnel. The Centurions form an international society, and a United States branch, the Society of Centurions of America, was founded by Joan Appleton in 1996.

Some Centurions speak publicly of their journey into the abortion industry, and how by grace they were rescued from it. But that is not the focus of the Society. The focus, rather, is their own personal healing. Periodically, Centurions from around the world come together, and under the expert guidance of Dr. Philip Ney, a practicing child and family psychiatrist, walk the long and painful road toward healing. Dr. Ney has written a fascinating book, *The Centurion's Pathway,* describing this road. He explains how the wounds of personal abuse often pave the way for a person to abuse others by practicing abortion. He also describes how former providers need to personalize each of the children they have destroyed. Some, for example, will name and even make illustrations of each of the children they were responsible for aborting.

My friend Joan Appleton, who was once the head nurse of an abortion facility in Falls Church, VA and started the American version of the Society of Centurions in 1996, continues to build this ministry through her own one-on-one counseling. Her email is joan.appleton@plan.org. She has written an account of her own journey, called *Raising Cecilia.*

The Centurions' brochure puts it beautifully:

"The Centurion who stood at the foot of the cross of Christ suddenly became horrified at the crucifixion he was ordered to carry out. When Christ died, this Centurion dropped his sword and fell to his knees exclaiming, 'Surely, this was an innocent man!'

"Those of us who have participated in the killing of unborn children are the Centurions of today. We have dropped our swords against the unborn child. Now we must recognize the depth of our guilt and deal with the ramifications . . . To revitalize our humanity we need to forgive and be forgiven, to reconcile and be healed."

May it be so, Amen!

For more information about the Society of Centurions of America visit www.priestsforlife.org.

Should We Talk with Abortionists?

ONE of my favorite pro-life activities is to actually sit down and talk with abortion providers.

Though this is hard for some to understand, the whole context of God's dealings with sinful humanity is known as the "dialogue of salvation" (See Vatican II, *Constitution on the Church in the Modern World* #3, #23; Pope Paul VI, *Ecclesiam Suam*). Dialogue acknowledges the human dignity of both parties, a dignity which is not lost even by a murderer (See *The Gospel of Life*, #9).

Two extreme positions need to be avoided.

The first is the idea that dialogue is useless or is a betrayal of the pro-life cause. It is not useless. Dialogue helps clear up misunderstandings and prejudices, even if it does not result in agreement. I have seen abortion supporters became aware, for the first time, of pro-life efforts to help women in crisis pregnancies, and of the difference between rejecting someone's actions and rejecting the person.

Nor is dialogue a betrayal of the pro-life cause. Discussing one's position does not require softening the position. Dialogue is not meant to look for some "compromise" between "pro-life" and "pro-choice." There is none. It does not seek a society that can encompass both a pro-life and abortion-rights philosophy. Such a society cannot survive.

Instead, dialogue seeks to communicate the truth, to help people understand each other, and to create the climate in which truth can best be accepted and flourish.

Dialogue has value.

The other extreme is to overestimate or oversimplify

that value, thinking that dialogue will solve everything or that it is the only legitimate response to the abortion crisis. Dialogue will not solve everything. In some cases, promoters of abortion will show no interest whatsoever in talking with pro-lifers.

Dialogue, even under the best circumstances, is by no means the only legitimate pro-life activity. "Let us love not in word or speech", St. John says, "but in deed and truth" (1 Jn 3:18). Abortion is not merely an "issue" or a "controversy," it is a tragedy, and it has victims. The victims need a defense, and they need it today. They cannot wait until everyone agrees to defend them.

Dialogue does, however, need to be practiced more frequently. Pro-life groups and individuals should invite abortionists and abortion rights supporters to talk. Pro-life training seminars should include training on how to talk with them effectively. Numerous conversions from the pro-abortion ranks to pro-life ranks have occurred as a result of the communications, respect, and love that pro-lifers have offered. The reason is that the best way to convince someone of the dignity of human life is to treat him/her with dignity. Many think the preborn have no value because they think that their own lives have no value. Many trample on the preborn only after having been trampled upon themselves. The only way our message will get through to some of these people is if we treat them with such respect that they think, "My life has some value." In discovering that value, they might then find it easier to discover it again in the babies.

The Conversion of Norma McCorvey

TRUTH and sin have very little in common, but there is one characteristic they both seem to share: start flirting with either one of them, and they draw you all the way in.

Norma McCorvey's life and conversion, so powerfully summarized in her recent book *Won by Love,* illustrate this truth dramatically. The deceit of the abortion industry drew her in and brought her to the depths of anguish, misery, and confusion. Then she began flirting with the truth, a little here and a little there. She listened to my good friend, Rev. Flip Benham, admit in all humility that he too needs God's forgiveness, and thus she allowed her stereotype of pro-life people as "self-righteous" to crumble. She listened to a little girl invite her to come to church, and finally (after many invitations) thought it would do no harm to check it out. Little by little, truth drew her in and proved itself more attractive than the abortion industry.

She finally accepted Christ in faith, was baptized, and became a believer. At the beginning, however, she still thought some early abortions would be acceptable. She was open to truth, however, and truth did not let her go. It drew her further, and she quickly became convinced that abortion is wrong at any stage, no matter what the reason. She even wears a T-shirt at pro-life gatherings that says "100% Pro-life, Without Exception, Without Compromise, Without Apology."

The truth has continued to draw Norma further. In my contacts with her over recent years, I noticed her interest in Catholicism. Shortly after her baptism, she asked me to bless her home. (Not being used to the custom of Holy

Water, she and her friend inadvertently drank the entire spare supply I left with them.) She attended with interest a Mass I celebrated in Dallas, and the following summer came with me to EWTN to tape a television interview. In the course of that interview, she asked me to bless the cross she wears, a cross which was made out of what used to be a pro-choice bracelet.

At one point, Norma asked me to teach her to say the Rosary. As we continued to talk about her faith, I realized she felt very strongly the call to fully embrace Catholicism. I simply answered her questions, which she raised in her own time and her own way. Then one day she sent me an email in which she told me that "The Big Boss" told her she was to join the Church.

Norma is now a practicing Catholic. The warm embrace which the Church extends to her is a sign of hope to everyone, but I especially see it as a sign of hope to our brothers and sisters who are still enmeshed in the abortion industry. We vigorously oppose what they do, but we do not hate them. We embrace them, too. The door of the Church is open. Truth continues to lead her children forward.

Roe's Companion

"I'VE been pro-life from day one. I don't believe in abortion—it's against my wishes. I never wanted an abortion and never went for one."

Believe it or not, those are words spoken by the plaintiff in one of the two companion abortion decisions of the United States Supreme Court which legalized abortion throughout the 50 states and throughout the pregnancy.

January 22 is marked each year by the remembrance of the 1973 *Roe vs. Wade* decision. But *Roe vs. Wade* was not the only decision on abortion issued that day. The Supreme Court issued a companion decision, *Doe vs. Bolton,* which is meant to be read in conjunction with *Roe vs. Wade.* The plaintiff was Sandra Cano. She describes January 22 not as a day of victory, even though she "won" the case, but as a day of tragic sadness for her and the babies. She is so deeply opposed to abortion that she wants the case re-opened and her name—as well as the lies associated with it—purged from the records.

Roe vs. Wade said the only abortions the state could prohibit, if it wanted, were abortions in the third trimester provided they were not necessary for the woman's life or health. The exact words of the Court are, "For the stage subsequent to viability the State, in promoting its interest in the potentiality of human life, may, if it chooses, regulate, and even proscribe, abortion except where it is necessary, in appropriate medical judgment, for the preservation of the life or health of the mother" (*Roe,* 410 U.S. at 164-65).

In the companion case of *Doe vs. Bolton,* the Court defined the scope of the "health" exception as follows:

"The medical judgment may be exercised in the light of all factors—physical, emotional, psychological, familial, and the woman's age—relevant to the well-being of the patient. All these factors may relate to health" (*Doe*, 410 U.S. at 192).

What this means, as the analysis of the University of Detroit Law Review points out, is that the Supreme Court's decisions "allowed abortion on demand throughout the entire nine months of pregnancy" (Vol. 67, Issue 2, p.157, note 3).

And all based on lies.

When Sandra Cano of Atlanta, Georgia approached her attorneys for help, she understood her case as an effort to obtain a divorce and regain custody of her children. She was pregnant, and her attorney, in partnership with Sandra's mother, arranged an abortion for Sandra at Georgia Baptist Hospital. Sandra had no knowledge of this plan. Such an act was so far from her intentions that when Sandra finally found out about it, she fled to Oklahoma alone.

On March 23, 1997, Sandra Cano joined Norma McCorvey (the plaintiff in *Roe vs. Wade*) at the National Memorial for the Unborn at Chattanooga, Tennessee, where they both publicly renounced their role in these abortion decisions. Her words are a sign of lasting hope for our nation: "I pledge that as long as I have breath, I will strive to see abortion ended in America."

Publicly Calling Abortionists to Repent

ONE of the most effective ways to stop abortion is to dry up the supply of abortion providers. This happens to a large extent by itself, as the already relatively small band of abortionists grows older and young doctors seem more reluctant to use their skills to destroy babies. However, the abortion industry aggressively recruits doctors for its purposes. Incidentally, this is a major reason for their push toward chemical abortions.

There are a number of things the pro-life movement can do to see to it that although abortion is legal, fewer and fewer people will be willing to provide it.

One of those things is actually a very old practice in the Christian world: admonish the sinner. This is one of the spiritual works of mercy. An aspect of charity is to alert the sinner to the harm that sin does to him/her, as well as to the victim. In fact, the Second Vatican Council, in the *Pastoral Constitution on the Church in the Modern World*, says that crimes like abortion do more harm to those who practice them than to the victims themselves!

Abortion is a public activity, and is publicly advertised. There is nothing against charity to publicly call for prayers for the abortion provider, by name, and to publicly call upon the abortionist to repent.

The demands of charity in this case include being absolutely sure that the person in question does in fact provide abortions, and saying nothing untrue about the person. They also include making it clear that we in the pro-life movement and the Church always have the door open to those ready to repent of child-killing, as so many have already done. Approaching the individual, and providing opportunities for confidential dialog, are activities that also need to be included.

Besides the repentance of the individual, however, there is another side to the activity of publicly admonishing abortionists that the Church cannot afford to ignore. Even when a particular abortion provider does not repent, the public identification of that person as an abortionist sends a clear signal to other abortionists and to those in medical school who might consider becoming abortionists: Perform this activity, and you will face the spotlight, with all the discomfort that entails! We have evidence that this works in dissuading actual and potential abortion providers.

One thing the abortion movement can never do is to remove the stigma from abortion. When we point out that specific people perform abortions, we capitalize on the biggest weakness of the other side.

It is interesting that many who perform abortions do not want to be called abortionists. Those who practice psychology are called psychologists. Those who practice neurology are called neurologists. There is nothing unusual, therefore, if we call those who practice abortion abortionists. The difference, of course, is that abortion carries a stigma which no amount of money or power can take away. That is a fact we should use to our advantage.

Inciting Violence?

STATES all over the country have passed bans on the partial-birth abortion procedure. Legislators in some states, like Missouri, voted to override their Governor's veto of such legislation.

The next step on the part of pro-abortion forces was to use the Court system to stop the law from taking effect. (Supporters of abortion know that they cannot get support for their extreme views from the public, so seek help from a handful of judges instead.)

What should really catch our attention, though, is one of the reasons that the Governor of Missouri gave for his veto of the partial-birth abortion ban. The Governor was reported to say that the legislation would constitute an open invitation to violence against abortion providers.

Now let me get this straight.

Legislation which prohibits an act of violence against a baby is bad, because it invites people to kill those who kill the baby? I wonder how many other acts of violence should therefore be permitted under law so that people won't feel justified in killing those who carry them out. This is upside-down thinking if there ever was such a thing.

Abortion supporters have been using this line for a while. I myself have been accused of inflaming violence simply because I write and preach that abortion is "killing."

Let's go back a few decades in history. When Rev. Martin Luther King, Jr. was exposing racial injustice and mobilizing people to correct it, he received a letter from eight Alabama clergymen. Part of the letter read,

"Just as we formerly pointed out that 'hatred and violence have no sanction in our religious and political traditions,' we also point out that such actions as incite to hatred and violence, however technically peaceful those actions may be, have not contributed to the resolution of our local problems."

Dr. King responded with his famous "Letter from a Birmingham Jail," in which he wrote,

"In your statement you assert that our actions, even though peaceful, must be condemned because they precipitate violence. But is this a logical assertion? Isn't this like condemning a robbed man because his possession of money precipitated the evil act of robbery? Isn't this like condemning Socrates because his unswerving commitment to truth and his philosophical inquiries precipitated the act by the misguided populace in which they made him drink hemlock? Isn't this like condemning Jesus because his unique God-consciousness and never-ceasing devotion to God's will precipitated the evil act of crucifixion? We must come to see that, as the Federal courts have consistently affirmed, it is wrong to urge an individual to cease his efforts to gain his basic constitutional rights because the quest may precipitate violence. Society must protect the robbed and punish the robber."

In our day, what actually promotes violence is the pro-choice mentality. When someone kills an abortion provider, he/she is practicing what pro-choicers have preached for decades: that sometimes it is OK to choose to end a life to solve a problem.

Denouncing Violence

PRIESTS for Life denounces the incidents of violence that have occurred against abortion providers. Echoing Pope John Paul II, we declare that "not even a murderer loses his personal dignity"(EV #9).

We also denounce the efforts continuously made by abortion advocates to blame pro-life groups for that violence. If anything, the violence done against abortionists is encouraged by the mentality and actions of those who promote abortion. Briefly, here's why.

First of all, for over 25 years, the so-called "pro-choice" mentality has been telling us that sometimes it's OK to choose to end a life to solve a problem. Though some try to defend abortion by saying "It's not a human life," more and more—both on the streets and in leadership—are abandoning that line of reasoning and admitting that abortion takes a human life. Naomi Wolfe wrote along these lines in her *New Republic* article "Our Bodies, Our Souls," and the same thinking was conveyed to me on the street by a man supporting abortion rights by holding a sign saying "Keep Baby-Killing Legal."

Besides the dangerous pro-choice rhetoric, the constant efforts of abortion supporters to suppress peaceful pro-life activity contributes to a "pressure-cooker" effect in society that can lead to violence. The FACE law (Freedom of Access to Clinic Entrances) signed by President Clinton in 1994, for example, does not simply punish violent activity. It also punishes the perfectly peaceful activity of blockading a doorway into which another human being is going to be brought to be killed. Whether one agrees with the strategy or not is beside the point. The point is that what the person does in that instance is peaceful. The law now treats it as criminal.

President John F. Kennedy once said that if you make peaceful protest impossible, you make violent protest inevitable. I found it interesting, for example, to read the story of Richard Andrews, who admitted to setting fire to seven abortion facilities. In the 1980s, this man peacefully and prayerfully blockaded the entrances to these facilities. His violent activity did not start until after something changed in the early 1990s—namely, a group of Washington facilities successfully sued to stop the blockades. This, of course, does not prove anything. But it would be shortsighted not to include this dynamic in our evaluation of the causes of violence against abortion providers.

All violence must be opposed, whatever one's beliefs about social issues. The government and the abortion supporters will agree with these words. Bill Lann Lee, for instance, as acting attorney general for civil rights stated, "Even those who disagree [with abortion rights] must agree that the violent destruction of property has no place in our society." Dr. Garson Romalis, himself wounded in an attack, said, "No matter what people's beliefs are with regard to the abortion issue, the shooting of a doctor is a violent act. It's a terrorist act."

We agree.

But then we also wonder why, at the same time, one's "belief" that abortion is justifiable takes precedence over that fact that it, too, is a violent act.

Part VII

The Government

Caesar Must Obey God

AN important theme of Old Testament history is the way in which God's people Israel related to the other nations surrounding them. The people of the covenant were not to follow the idolatrous practices of those nations. Israel, after all, had the benefit of God's revealed law. The other nations did not.

One thing that the Israelites wanted to imitate, however, was the fact that other nations had a king. At one point they demanded of Samuel the prophet, "Give us a king!" Upon consulting the Lord, Samuel was told, "They have asked for a king—Give them a king." But God also gave this essential warning: both the people and their king have a king in heaven! The well-being of the entire nation depends on the obedience which both the king and his people give to the King of heaven. (See 1 Sam 8:1-22 and 12:13-15.)

The Lord Jesus expressed the same theme in Matthew 22:15-22. When asked whether taxes should be paid to Caesar, Jesus asked whose image and inscription was on the coin. "Caesar's," came the answer. The Lord then said, "Give to Caesar what is due to Caesar, and to God what is due to God" (Mt 22:21).

The coin belongs to Caesar, for it bears Caesar's image. Human beings belong to God, for they bear God's image! The implication of the passage is that "What belongs to God" includes Caesar himself! Caesar must obey God.

Both the passage from 1Samuel and from Matthew's Gospel teach what the Second Vatican Council commented upon at length, namely, that separation of Church and state does not mean separation of God and state. If you separate the state from God, the State disintegrates. While the Church does not have a political mission, she nevertheless has a political responsibility: to bear witness to those moral truths without which the common good—which is the very purpose for which governments are instituted—cannot survive. These moral truths are basic and go beyond the bounds of any denominational beliefs. Because they are truths, they must shape public policy.

Not only do individuals have a duty to obey God, but so do governments.

Christians have a duty to be politically active, to register and vote, to lobby and educate candidates and elected officials, and to speak up about the issues that affect the common good. The Church does not set up the voting booths, but when we go into the voting booths, we don't cease to be members of the Church! If we don't shape public policy according to moral truths, why do we believe that moral truth at all?

Now is the time, now is the challenge. No longer are we to think of our religion as a purely "private matter." Christ taught in public and He was crucified in public. Now risen from the dead, He places us in the public arena, with the commission to make disciples of all nations (See Mt 28:18-20). May we not fail Him or our nation.

You Wouldn't Even Ask

IF a candidate who supported terrorism asked for your vote, would you say, "I disagree with you on terrorism, but where do you stand on other issues?"

I doubt it.

In fact, if a terrorism sympathizer presented him/herself for your vote, you would immediately know that such a position disqualifies the candidate for public office—no matter how good he or she may be on other issues. The horror of terrorism dwarfs whatever good might be found in the candidate's plan for housing, education, or health care. Regarding those plans, you wouldn't even ask.

So why do so many people say, "This candidate favors legal abortion. I disagree. But I'm voting for this person because she has good ideas about health care (or some other issue)."

Such a position makes no sense whatsoever, unless one is completely blind to the violence of abortion. That, of course, is the problem. But we need only see what abortion looks like, or read descriptions from the abortionists themselves, and the evidence is clear. (*USA Today* refused to sell me space for an ad that quoted abortionists describing their work because the readers would be traumatized just by the words!)

Abortion is no less violent than terrorism. Any candidate who says abortion should be kept legal disqualifies him/herself from public service. We need look no further, we need pay no attention to what that candidate says on other issues. Support for abortion is enough for us to decide not to vote for such a person.

Pope John Paul II put it this way: "Above all, the common outcry, which is justly made on behalf of human rights—for example, the right to health, to home, to work, to family, to culture—is false and illusory if the right to life, the most basic and fundamental right and the condition for all other personal rights, is not defended with maximum determination" (*Christifideles Laici*, 1988).

False and illusory. Those are strong and clear words that call for our further reflection.

"I stand for adequate and comprehensive health care." So far, so good. But as soon as you say that a procedure that tears the arms off of little babies is part of "health care," then your understanding of the term "health care" is obviously quite different from the actual meaning of the words. In short, you lose credibility. Your claim to health care is "illusory." It sounds good, but is in fact destructive, because it masks an act of violence.

"My plan for adequate housing will succeed." Fine. But what are houses for, if not for people to live in them? If you allow the killing of the children who would otherwise live in those houses, how am I supposed to get excited by your housing project?

It's easy to get confused by all the arguments. But if you start by asking where candidates stand on abortion, you can eliminate a lot of other questions you needn't even ask.

For more election related articles and information, visit www.priestsforlife.org/elections.

Sinful Voting

CAN you commit a sin in the voting booth?

Morality has to do with human activity and human choices. Any time we make any kind of decision about what we do, say, or even think, we are either affirming or denying the moral law, and therefore are either coming closer to God or going farther away from him. Every step we take on the journey of life either strengthens us in virtue or enslaves us in vice.

Wherever we are, then, it is possible to perform a virtuous act or to commit a sin. I may be singing God's praises in the choir amidst a splendid liturgy—but if I deliberately think thoughts of rash judgment against a fellow choir member, I have sinned in the midst of those holy surroundings. Conversely, I may be a police officer called to investigate a complaint inside a nightclub where immoral acts are being committed at every turn. By carrying out my duty diligently, however, I can perform virtuous acts despite the surroundings. In short, the only "no-virtue" or "no-sin" zones are on the other side of the grave.

Now sin or virtue is always a combination of my action, my intention, and the circumstances surrounding both. I cannot tell whether a photo of two men carrying a TV set out of an apartment is the photo of sin or virtue, because I don't know if they are two thieves or two repairmen. All the relevant facts have to be considered, and not all of those facts are always available.

Let's look at one example of a voting booth sin. A voter believes in "abortion rights," and for that reason knowingly and deliberately votes for a candidate who has promised to protect those "rights." That is a sin. The voter has intentionally helped someone who is attempting to advance a violent and destructive activity. The vote in that case is similar to the sinful act of taking part in a pro-abortion rally, writing an editorial letter that expresses support for abortion, or otherwise encouraging or enabling those who perform abortions.

To say this has nothing to do with being partisan, because anybody of any party at any time might take any position on abortion, and yet this teaching remains the same. Nor is it "telling people how to vote," but rather pointing out the moral implications of voting.

Evaluating Issues

IN an election season, Catholics are called upon to evaluate a wide range of issues as they determine what candidates they will support.

We who are leaders in the pro-life movement do not say that abortion is the only issue. It is, however, the foundational issue. Many things destroy human life. Yet abortion goes beyond that. Our nation's current abortion policy authorizes such destruction, by a direct denial of the protections granted to persons under the US Constitution.

An example will clarify this. We are rightly concerned about the poor, and need to develop programs and policies to advance their rights and enhance their lives. Sometimes people are heard to say that offenses against the poor are a more compelling concern to them than the abortion problem. Certainly, the problems are related, because a consistent ethic of life recognizes that human life is sacred always and everywhere, and that progress in any area of advancing human dignity means progress in all the other areas as well.

But to make a truly equivalent parallel between the plight of the poor and that of the unborn, one would have to imagine a policy whereby a) the poor were officially declared to be devoid of "personhood" under the Constitution (as *Roe vs. Wade* did to the unborn), and b) over 4,000 of the poor were put to death daily against their will, while efforts to directly save them were prosecuted by the government (as is the case regarding the unborn).

It is one thing to assert that a particular policy does or does not advance the rights of the poor; it is quite another to assert that the poor have no right to exist. Debates about the poor are in the first category; the debate about the unborn is in the second.

In their 1989 *Resolution on Abortion,* the US bishops therefore declared, "At this particular time, abortion has become the fundamental human rights issue for all men and women of good will."

In their 1998 statement *Living the Gospel of Life,* the bishops likewise explained, "Opposition to abortion and euthanasia does not excuse indifference to those who suffer from poverty, violence and injustice. . . . Therefore, Catholics should eagerly involve themselves as advocates for the weak and marginalized in all these areas. Catholic public officials are obliged to address each of these issues . . . But being 'right' in such matters can never excuse a wrong choice regarding direct attacks on innocent human life. Indeed, the failure to protect and defend life in its most vulnerable stages renders suspect any claims to the 'rightness' of positions in other matters affecting the poorest and least powerful of the human community. If we understand the human person as the 'temple of the Holy Spirit'—the living house of God—then these latter issues fall logically into place as the crossbeams and walls of that house. All direct attacks on innocent human life, such as abortion and euthanasia, strike at the house's foundation" (n. 23).

Elections and the Consistent Ethic

THE Church embraces a consistent ethic of life. In their 1999 statement "Faithful Citizenship," the Administrative Committee of the USCC stated, "We are convinced that a consistent ethic of life should be the moral framework from which to address all issues in the political arena." The consistent ethic acknowledges that while individual issues affecting human dignity are unique, they are interrelated to the point where progress on one front affects progress on all fronts.

"Faithful Citizenship" belongs to a line of statements on political responsibility issued every four years since the mid-1970s. In 1984, Joseph Cardinal Bernardin, the most well-known spokesperson regarding the consistent ethic of life, had this to say about the role of such statements: "The purpose is surely not to tell citizens how to vote, but to help shape the public debate and form personal conscience so that every citizen will vote thoughtfully and responsibly. Our 'Statement on Political Responsibility' has always been, like our 'Respect Life Program,' a multi-issue approach to public morality. The fact that this Statement sets forth a spectrum of issues of current concern to the Church and society should not be understood as implying that all issues are qualitatively equal from a moral perspective . . . As I indicated earlier, each of the life issues—while related to all the others—is distinct and calls for its own specific moral analysis." (*A Consistent Ethic of Life: Continuing the Dialogue*, The William Wade Lecture Series, St. Louis University, March 11, 1984).

Notice that the Cardinal stated that not all issues are qualitatively equal from a moral perspective. A consistent ethic recognizes that there is justification for placing priority emphasis on certain issues at certain times. Hence, the document "Faithful Citizenship" goes on to say, "Our world does not lack for threats to human life. We watch with horror the deadly violence of war, genocide and massive starvation in other lands, and children dying from lack of adequate health care. Yet as we wrote in our 1998 statement, *Living the Gospel of Life,* 'Abortion and euthanasia have become preeminent threats to human life and dignity because they directly attack life itself, the most fundamental good and the condition for all others.' "

To ignore the priority attention that the problems of abortion and euthanasia demand is to misunderstand both the consistent ethic and the nature of the threats that these evils pose. On Respect Life Sunday, October 1, 1989, Cardinal Bernardin issued a statement entitled "Deciding for Life," in which he said, "Not all values, however, are of equal weight. Some are more fundamental than others. On this Respect Life Sunday, I wish to emphasize that no earthly value is more fundamental than human life itself. Human life is the condition for enjoying freedom and all other values. Consequently, if one must choose between protecting or serving lesser human values that depend upon life for their existence and life itself, human life must take precedence."

The False Dichotomy of Pro-Choice Politicians

"IT has been a particular sadness to the bishops of the United States and to Catholics active in the pro-life movement that so many Catholic politicians have succumbed to the pressures exerted by pro abortion advocates. Many of these politicians resort to the explanation that they are personally opposed to abortion, but they do not feel that they can impose their own moral judgment upon others. Again and again the Bishops of the United States have attempted, both collectively and individually, to disabuse politicians of this false dichotomy."

Thus spoke Bernard Cardinal Law on October 23, 1998, at a meeting of European politicians and legislators convened by the Pontifical Council for the Family, Vatican City.

Having preached to, listened to, and worked with such pro-life people in every state in the nation, I for one can certainly attest to the existence of this sadness among Catholics active in the pro-life movement.

One man on the street put it simply and effectively when he asked me, "Father, if that politician can't respect the life of a little baby, how can I expect him to respect mine?"

Good question.

I have posed it, in other words, to officials at the highest levels of our government. What issue, I have repeatedly asked, is more fundamental to those who govern the political community than that of who belongs to the political community? How can a public servant claim to serve the public and ignore the systematic destruction of a whole segment of the public he claims to serve?

"We have to govern everybody," some say in their defense.

That is our point precisely. That is why we oppose a Supreme Court decision that says, "The word 'person', as used in the Fourteenth Amendment, does not include the unborn." (*Roe vs. Wade,* at 158).

"The government shouldn't be involved in abortion," others claim.

In fact, the government became too involved in abortion when, in 1973, it overstepped its authority and asserted that it could decide who has the right to live and who doesn't. It you want the government out of abortion, then tell the government to back off and stop pretending that it is the source of the right to life. Let it start acting as the guardian of that right instead.

"The law shouldn't impose religious beliefs."

We don't want it to. The law that says you can't take my life does not require you to believe anything about my life. It just says you can't take it. All the pro-life movement is saying is to extend that protection equally to all members of the human species.

"There are many issues."

Of course there are, and the reason is that human life and dignity is threatened in many ways. Deny the equal right to life of all, however, and you undermine every legitimate cause at the same time.

"Personally opposed but . . ." A false dichotomy, indeed.

Legislating Morality

SOME declare that "you can't legislate morality." Let's look more closely at what that statement means.

If it means the law is not sufficient to make everyone morally responsible, that is certainly true. We need more than laws to make people good. Their hearts and minds need to be converted. Laws do have both a teaching and restraining function, however, that actually keep people within the bounds of moral behavior, even if unwillingly. As Rev. Dr. Martin Luther King, Jr. observed, the law can't make my brother love me, but it can keep him from lynching me.

If the phrase means the law is not the source of morality, that is also true. Morality comes not from law, but from the nature of the human person, which ultimately flows from the nature of God.

If the phrase means laws have nothing to do with morality, as if there is a total separation between one's "moral life" and one's "social life," this is patently false. This is the idea that whatever a law says is OK is OK. In reality, however, majorities can be wrong. Furthermore, both morality and law deal with human behavior. Any time you legislate the boundaries of human behavior, you are legislating morality.

It seems that the "you can't legislate morality" argument arises most often when the Church speaks up for the right to life of every human person, from conception to natural death, and when the Church insists that such a right must be protected by law. The US bishops did this quite eloquently in their document *Living the Gospel of Life: A Challenge to American Catholics* (1998). Commenting on the criticism that often follows such assertions, Cardinal John O'Connor once wrote, "Why are bishops criticized only when the public policy question involves abortion? Why would I be praised for encouraging the mayor, the governor, the Congress and the president to intensify the war on drugs, but criticized if I urge the same regarding abortion?" ("Abortion: Questions and Answers," 1990).

No issue is more fundamental than the right to life.

"In an age of artifice, many voters are hungry for substance. They admire and support political figures who speak out sincerely for their moral convictions. For our part we commend Catholic and other public officials who, with courage and determination, use their positions of leadership to promote respect for all human life" (US Bishops, *Living the Gospel of Life*, 1998, n. 31).

An election cycle is no time for silence. "American Catholics have long sought to assimilate into U.S. cultural life. But in assimilating, we have too often been digested. We have been changed by our culture too much, and we have changed it not enough. If we are leaven, we must bring to our culture the whole Gospel, which is a Gospel of life and joy. That is our vocation as believers. And there is no better place to start than promoting the beauty and sanctity of human life" (ibid, n. 25).

God's Dominion

IT is not surprising, in post-election analysis, that those who worship regularly tend to vote for pro-life candidates. The attitude of worship is directly contrary to that of "pro-choice."

Worship says, "God is the Lord of my choices." The "pro-choice" mentality is, "I am the Lord of my choices. Whatever I decide is right, is right for me." The whole teaching of the Gospel, of course, is that authentic freedom is found in submitting ourselves to the Lordship of Christ. Ultimately, the struggle over abortion is a struggle over the sovereignty of God.

In fact, the dominion of God over human life is the key doctrine on which the Church's opposition to abortion rests. This is more precisely the foundation, rather than any position about when the soul is created and infused into the body. Some proponents of abortion point to various theological positions through the centuries which placed "ensoulment" at different points after conception, and thus regarded abortion as a different kind of offense depending on when it was performed. The two points to keep in mind when you hear this are that first, abortion was always regarded as wrong, no matter what kind of wrong it was classified as. Second, the basis for saying it is wrong is that God alone is Lord of Life; He alone gives it, sustains it, and takes it to Himself.

It is in this doctrine, moreover, that we find the basis for the Church's opposition also to artificial contraception, infanticide, and euthanasia. God alone has dominion over human life and over the entire process of its coming to be. Pope John Paul II described, in *Evangelium Vitae,* that abortion and contraception are related "as fruits of the same tree." That tree is the separation of our freedom from the dominion of God and His truth.

We also find here a key to resolving what many find to be an apparent contradiction: the Church's opposition to abortion and contraception on the one hand, and to artificial reproduction on the other. If the Church is for life, they ask, why does it oppose artificial reproduction? The answer is that the process and fruit of reproduction is the gift of a human person rather than a "product" of human ingenuity and skill. As a gift, given by a sovereign God, a new life can neither be destroyed nor demanded.

I was once praying at an abortion facility with a group of pro-life activists and the diocesan respect life director of the area. One man had his toes over the property line of the facility, and someone on the inside yelled, "Get your feet off our property!" He politely complied. I then asked aloud to the workers in the facility, "And when are you going to get your hands off God's property?"

He indeed has dominion. May we, in freely assenting to it, find our true and only fulfillment.

Roe *Can* Fall

STUDY constitutional history, and you can conclude that the days of *Roe vs. Wade* are numbered. The reason is that the foundation of the Constitution itself, and the direction of its history, is the recognition of the equal dignity of those who, at various times, were deprived of their rights and suffered violence which was given legal cover under a different name. This legal cover was often mistakenly recognized by the Supreme Court for a while, but then such decisions were overturned.

Dred Scott v. Sandford (1856) is the most commonly cited instance. The slaveholder's right to property eclipsed and subsumed the slave's right to freedom. But the Constitution was eventually amended to correct the error.

Decisions like *Lochner v. New York* (1905) show us another error: employers' right to contract eclipsed and subsumed the workers' rights to humane conditions and hours. These abuses were corrected by subsequent Supreme Court decisions like *Muller v. Oregon* and *Bunting v. Oregon*.

The "Separate but equal" doctrine of *Plessy v. Ferguson* (1896) sanctioning segregation was overturned by *Brown v. Board of Education* some 58 years later.

Erroneous decisions like *Hammer v. Dagenhart* (1918) institutionalized child labor. But this was overturned 23 years later by *United States v. Darby*. A new development—a "pedagogical moment"—occurred here in constitutional law. The question was whether constitutional rights applied to children too. The answer was yes.

Now it is time for the "embryonic moment," the recognition that the rights of the Constitution apply also to the unborn child. Until *Roe,* only state law addressed the unborn. Now their status has become a constitutional issue, and must be developed by using constitutional principles. Once again, an act of violence is given legal cover by some other right, in this case the "right to privacy."

Constitutionally, there is no precedent on abortion. A concept could be used, however, from the "Law of Bailments," which is defined as the "divided dominion" of personal property which contemplates custody in one part and ownership in another. When you deposit your money in the bank, you have absolute dominion over it, while the bank has a "trust-dominion."

Analogously, the child *in utero* has absolute dominion over his/her own person. The mother has a trust dominion rather than an absolute dominion that would allow her to destroy the child.

Many reversals of Supreme Court cases came about when new evidence was brought forward that made it clear that someone's rights, not previously recognized, were being violated. Thus, Louis Brandeis brought forward the facts about how workers were being harmed. With some 200 embryological sciences, such evidence, combined with new legal concepts, can challenge *Roe* in the same way its erroneous ancestral decisions were challenged.

Fr. Clifford Stevens, a priest of the Omaha Archdiocese, founded the National Organization for Embryonic Law to conduct the kind of research I have traced above, and to call for attorneys to seize the "embryonic moment" of constitutional history that we are now in. The research can be found on our website, www.priestsforlife.org. Judging from past constitutional history, *Roe* will go the way of other discarded lies.

Three Branches

IF you take a tour of the US Capitol in Washington, DC, you eventually reach a relatively small room in the basement. It is the old Supreme Court. Prior to getting its own building across the street, the Supreme Court used to be housed under the building in which our federal lawmakers gather, deliberate, and vote. The symbolic significance of this, of course, is that we govern ourselves. Our elected representatives, who are accountable to us, pass laws. Judges don't. They simply judge whether an existing law has been violated in a particular case, by particular parties.

Or at least that's what they're supposed to do.

We live in an age of judicial activism, or as some have called it, judicial tyranny. Judges are striking down laws and writing new ones left and right, without precedent and without reason. For example, the Supreme Court decision *Engel v. Vitale* in 1962 attacked the longstanding tradition of school prayer, declaring that a voluntary, non-denominational prayer in a public school was unconstitutional. The Court failed to cite a single precedent to justify its prohibition. "For 170 years following the ratification of the Constitution and Bill of Rights, no Court had ever struck down any prayer, in any form, in any location" (Barton, *Original Intent*, p. 159).

Things went downhill from there, in many different decisions. In 1973, the *Roe v. Wade* and *Doe v. Bolton* decisions unleashed the abortion holocaust. In his dissent, Justice Byron White issued the famous assertion that the Court delivered "an exercise of raw judicial power . . . an improvident and extravagant exercise of the power of judicial review."

Now the Courts are tampering with the very nature of marriage as a union between man and woman.

The Founding Fathers knew the dangers of a Court system that would try to take control of the rest of the government. Thomas Jefferson wrote, "[T]he germ of dissolution of our federal government is in the constitution of the federal Judiciary; . . . working like gravity by night and by day, gaining a little today and a little tomorrow, and advancing its noiseless step like a thief, over the field of jurisdiction, until all shall be usurped" (Bergh, *Writings of Thomas Jefferson*, Vol. XV, pp. 331-332).

The Founders established three distinct branches of government—the legislative, executive, and judicial—and made it clear that "each of the three departments has equally the right to decide for itself what is its duty under the Constitution, without any regard to what the others may have decided for themselves under a similar question" (Thomas Jefferson, ibid., p.215). In other words, the President and members of Congress pledge to uphold the Constitution, not the Court's opinion of the Constitution.

Little by little, Americans are waking up to judicial tyranny, and are calling for a change. It is time to make this a key election issue and to choose leaders who understand that the people, not the courts, decide the direction our national policies will take.

Republic

"REMEMBER, democracy never lasts long. It soon wastes, exhausts, and murders itself. There never was a democracy yet that did not commit suicide."

That quote is not from an anarchist or a totalitarian leader. It is, perhaps surprisingly, from John Adams, the second President of the United States, and a signer of the Declaration of Independence.

Similar quotes can be found in the writings of other Founding Fathers of our nation, because although they had the opportunity to do so, they did not establish a democracy. What they established for America, instead, is a republic. And great is the difference between the two.

In a democracy, policies are made by a direct majority vote of the people. What the majority says, goes, and that is final and absolute. So, for example, if the majority were to say that murder is OK, it would be OK. There would not be a mechanism, in a pure democracy, to keep it from being OK, except that the majority changed its mind.

A republic, however, is based not on the rule of the majority, but on the rule of law. Representatives are elected, and they pass laws. They are accountable to the people, and in this sense majorities matter. But they are also accountable to a higher law, and there is the key difference. There are certain laws that the majority can never change. These laws flow from the fundamental rights of the human person and from God Himself.

The Founding Fathers recognized this and expected all future generations of Americans to recognize it as well. Alexander Hamilton, a signer of the Constitution, wrote, "[T]he law . . . dictated by God Himself is, of course, superior in obligation to any other. It is binding over all the globe, in all countries, and at all times. No human laws are of any validity if contrary to this" (*The Papers of Alexander Hamilton*, Vol. I, p. 87).

James Wilson, another signer of the Constitution and a US Supreme Court Justice, wrote, "All [laws], however, may be arranged in two different classes, 1) Divine 2) Human . . . Human law must rest its authority ultimately upon the authority of that law which is Divine" (*The Works of the Honourable James Wilson*, Vol. I, pp. 103-105).

The Founders of our nation believed in Biblical law, and that was the standard for law and government in our country until the turn of this century. Now, instead, legal positivism has become the standard. It says that there are no unchanging, superior laws. Rather, man-made law is the final law and can always change according to circumstances. That's the poisoned soil out of which *Roe vs. Wade* and other abortion decisions have grown.

It's time for a change. We need to re-discover our own history and impart it to our youth. The primary legal document of our nation, the Declaration of Independence, recognizes in its first sentence that "the laws of nature and of nature's God" are primary. We are not a democracy; we are a republic.

Free Speech in Church

THERE is a legitimate separation of Church and State. The Church cannot decide that there are 51 states instead of 50, nor can the State decide that there are 8 sacraments instead of 7. The mission of each is distinct, and as the Second Vatican Council teaches, "Christ did not bequeath to the Church a mission in the political, economic, or social order: the purpose he assigned to it was a religious one" (GS 42).

At the same time, the missions do overlap. ". . . At all times and in all places, the Church should have the true freedom to teach the faith, to proclaim its teaching about society, to carry out its task among men without hindrance, and to pass moral judgment even in matters relating to politics, whenever the fundamental rights of man or the salvation of souls requires it" (GS 76; cited in *Living the Gospel of Life*, US Bishops, 1998, n. 18).

This "true freedom" corresponds well to the vision of religious liberty on which America rests. The First Amendment forbids Congress from establishing a religion, or hindering its free exercise. The Supreme Court has often indicated that debate on public issues should be unhindered, robust, and wide-open.

Yet the Church is not as free as it might be in commenting on politics, because of regulations which the IRS places on tax-exempt organizations. These regulations prohibit political advocacy. Yes, we may address issues; no, we may not participate or intervene, directly or indirectly, in any political campaign on behalf of, or in opposition to, any candidate for public office.

And the problem is that what this means, in practice, isn't always so clear. The IRS takes a "facts and circumstances" approach to determining what constitutes a violation. In other words, a pastor may find out he is in violation only after the fact. This makes many pastors over-cautious.

The ban on political speech was inserted by Senator Lyndon Johnson as a floor amendment during debate on the 1954 Internal Revenue Code, in order to silence certain organizations that were opposing him. Not a single hearing took place nor was any congressional record developed to explain the reasons for the ban. There is no legislative history to clarify its meaning. Nor is there any indication that Senator Johnson intended to target houses of worship.

A bill has been introduced in Congress that may remedy this problem. HR 235, the Houses of Worship Free Speech Restoration Act, is simple straightforward legislation that will give back to churches the freedom to speak however they feel led to speak, whether the issue is construed as political or not. It amends section 501 of the IRS Code to say that Churches cannot be punished for political intervention "because of the content, preparation, or presentation of any homily, sermon, teaching, dialectic, or other presentation made during religious services or gatherings."

It makes sense to me. Religious leaders should have the right to speak from their heart, without fear of governmental stipulations.

Church Parking Lots

BEFORE general elections, many pastors are approached by people who wish to distribute campaign literature in the church parking lot, or who simply do it on their own.

These are people who have heard the call of the Church to get involved in transforming society! They have understood what the Second Vatican Council meant by the "apostolate of the laity" and their special call to be in the world as witnesses to Christ. They have learned what the Church teaches about the tragic separation of faith and life that leads many to worship in a corner but leave the world unchanged.

So they pay attention to elections. They find out who is running, and make a decision in conscience about who is the best person to exercise public office in a way that will advance God's Kingdom of justice, life, and peace. And now they take a practical step and attempt to inform their fellow-believers by handing out literature at the place where they are most likely to find them.

Then what happens? Often, they get thrown off the property! The very pastors who are ordained to stir up their gifts to get involved in changing the world now punish them for exercising those gifts!

There is no reason to throw such people off the property simply for putting literature on cars. Among the attorneys who advise us at Priests for Life are James Bopp, Jr. and Barry Bostrom, who are among the nation's leading experts on tax law and on what Churches are allowed to do regarding elections. In a recent letter, they advised us as follows:

". . . [T]he distribution of campaign material by others in the church parking lot will not jeopardize the church's tax exempt status. The mere permission of distribution of campaign materials by others in the church parking lot is not regulated by the Internal Revenue Code. The Code and its regulations are designed to limit only the activities and expenditures of non-profit organizations. Distribution of campaign materials by others outdoors, in a public parking lot, is not an activity or expenditure of the church . . .

". . . [I]n most states there are state court decisions holding that such activity is protected by the First Amendment to the U.S. Constitution and/or the State Constitution, and therefore, the church will suffer no adverse consequences as a result of this activity. There are many cases recognizing the free speech rights of individuals and protecting speech and petitioning, reasonably exercised, in public areas, even when the property is privately owned . . .

"In other words, churches not only may permit campaign statements to be distributed in their public parking lots, they cannot prohibit such distributions because the parking lots are open to the public."

I am grateful for this expert guidance.

Wouldn't it be great if we stopped worrying about what might happen if we do something, and started worrying about what might happen if we do nothing?

Separation of Church and State

PROMINENT pro-abortion politicians have often been heard repeating the message, "I don't tell Church leaders what to do, and Church leaders shouldn't tell public officials what to do." This is their considered summary of the "separation of Church and state."

Yet it seems that public officials have indeed told Church leaders what to do as the problems related to child sexual abuse by clergy have been addressed in the last couple of years. And in the course of addressing this problem, public officials are carrying out their duty. After all, they have to protect children, no matter who the abusers are.

The public officials addressing this problem are not telling the Church what to believe, what sacraments to administer, or what prayers and readings belong in the Sunday Mass. All these things and more are left to the proper Church authorities to administer, in a legitimate autonomy and "division of labor."

Yet obviously if Church leaders fail in the protection of innocent life, the state has the right and duty to step in. The state cannot pretend that it is free to ignore these abuses because of "separation of Church and state." Human suffering cannot be buried in abstractions.

The shoe also fits the other foot. While the Church does not make rules for mail delivery, or the delineation of county lines, or the administration of the army, the Church nevertheless does have some business telling the state a thing or two. This is especially true when the state is failing in its duty toward innocent children—or anyone else—in the matter of their fundamental human rights.

Again, human suffering cannot be buried in abstractions about "separation of Church and state." Both Church and state have the duty to defend human beings, and unless they uphold each other in that common task, neither can properly fulfill it.

People should always have freedom of belief. The truth that the Church proclaims has its own power to attract people to embrace it. Belief is not something to be imposed by law. Yet law must limit what the believer can do. What should we say about someone who kills you because he "doesn't believe" your life is valuable? It is not his belief that violated the law, but rather his action against you. Wouldn't public officials have to take a stand against that action, even while upholding the criminal's freedom of belief?

The killing of the unborn by abortion, because some don't believe that life is as valuable as yours or mine, is the most obvious battleground on this point.

A public official recently said that this is not "the Catholic Republic of America." I heartily agree. This is America, proud of its freedom of religion, and equally proud of its protection of human rights. The two can go together, as long as we realize that "separation of Church and state" can never mean that either one looks the other way when human rights are being violated.

Voter Registration Drives

IT IS perfectly legal for a Church to conduct a non-partisan voter registration campaign. "Non-partisan" means that it is not limited to people of any given party. In fact, nobody who is eligible under Federal and state law is excluded.

This activity simply consists of giving Church members the opportunity to fill out the voter registration forms at the back of Church. The forms take about a minute or two to complete.

Voter registration drives in the Churches are also fully consistent with the Gospel and with the call that the Pope and bishops have been making to us to get involved in the electoral process. Jesus commissioned his apostles to make disciples of all the nations and to teach them to carry out all His commands. The work of the Church is not simply to bring people to believe, but also to carry out the Lord's teachings. The Gospel transforms society and renews the face of the earth. That includes renewing the face of leadership, laws, policies, and political life.

Pope John Paul II, in his encyclical on the Eucharist, urged us not to neglect the duties of our citizenship, and the bishops remind us in *Living the Gospel of Life* that "every voice matters in the public forum; every vote counts."

So we are good to go, legally and spiritually. What keeps us from actually doing it?

One of the obstacles is an excessive fear that some dioceses and parishes have of working with "outside groups." Some, for example, may not want to do a "Christian Coalition" voter registration drive, or a

"Priests for Life" or "National Right to Life" voter registration drive.

Of course, parishes and dioceses are free to work with whom they choose. But that's not really the issue, because the decision not to work with a particular group does not absolve a Church of its duty to equip its members to be active voters. Voter registration drives are not inherently linked with any group. Voter registration is an activity that citizens do and that Churches have the right to facilitate. The activity is not owned by the Church or by any outside group. We at Priests for Life—along with many other national groups—promote awareness of the need to do voter registration, and share information on how to carry it out. It is the role of the local diocese and parish to then pick up the ball and run with it. If they are afraid to do so, they should admit that, rather than disguise their fear with the excuse that they cannot work with a particular group.

Meanwhile, we will not be afraid to call on everyone to register as many voters as possible—with or without the help of the Churches. Even night clubs have been conducting voter registration drives, to protect certain immoral activities. Will they do better than God's Church?

Useless Advice

"**WE** can't tell people how to vote."

I hear that phrase often. Some within the Church who say it think they are giving clear advice about what Churches—and other tax-exempt organizations—are restricted from doing.

But it's hardly clear advice. In fact, it's totally useless advice.

If we mean to say that Churches, under current law, cannot say "Vote for John Smith," then we should say, "Churches under current law cannot say 'Vote for John Smith.' "

But there are many other things Churches can say and have said. The United States Catholic Bishops, for example, wrote the following paragraph in their 1998 document *Living the Gospel of Life:*

"We encourage all citizens, particularly Catholics, to embrace their citizenship not merely as a duty and privilege, but as an opportunity meaningfully to participate in building the culture of life. Every voice matters in the public forum. Every vote counts. Every act of responsible citizenship is an exercise of significant individual power. We must exercise that power in ways that defend human life, especially those of God's children who are unborn, disabled or otherwise vulnerable. We get the public officials we deserve. Their virtue—or lack thereof—is a judgment not only on them, but on us. Because of this, we urge our fellow citizens to see beyond party politics, to analyze campaign rhetoric critically, and to choose their political leaders according to principle, not party affiliation or mere self-interest" (n. 34).

So did they "tell people how to vote" or not?

How about the following line from the Vatican's *Doctrinal Note on The Participation of Catholics in Political Life*: "A well-formed Christian conscience does not permit one to vote for a political program or an individual law which contradicts the fundamental contents of faith and morals" (n. 4).

Did the Vatican "tell people how to vote" or not?

Obviously, to assert that "we can't tell people how to vote" is so vague as to be meaningless. If we mean endorsing candidates, that's one thing. The Church as an institution cannot do that, but pastors and individual believers, as well as organizations not under the same restrictions, certainly can. It is, in fact, a spiritual work of mercy to inform one's neighbors about the candidates and urge them to vote for the best choice.

But short of making endorsements, the Church can and must give people moral guidance about how to vote, just as the Vatican and the United States bishops do in the quotes mentioned above. If we fail to give such guidance, we fail in our mission as the light of the world, and become as irrelevant as a lamp under a bushel basket.

Such a failure is especially grievous when our votes affect the lives and deaths of tens of millions of the most defenseless children, threatened by abortion. If the Church cannot speak at a time like this, what are the stones of our great buildings for, after all? Indeed, if we are silent, the very stones will cry out.

First, Be Reconciled

AN important perspective to consider on the question of whether pro-abortion politicians should receive communion is the teaching of Jesus about the need to reconcile with our brothers and sisters before coming to the altar.

"Therefore, if you are offering your gift at the altar and there remember that your brother has something against you, leave your gift there in front of the altar. First go and be reconciled to your brother; then come and offer your gift" (Mt 5:23-24).

Those who allow abortion are not reconciled with their unborn brothers and sisters. To fail to see the equal dignity of children in the womb with children outside the womb is prejudice. To consider the unborn as "non-persons" and unworthy of constitutional protection is an insult. And to consider one's unborn brothers and sisters as "tissue" or "parasites" is name-calling of the worst kind.

Those who do this have to go first and be reconciled with their unborn brothers and sisters before they can present their gift at the altar.

Communion is bestowed in the context of the Sacrifice of the Mass. That sacrifice is not only the sacrifice of Jesus, but of each of us along with Jesus. We offer him everything—our thoughts, our opinions, our relationships, our choices. We bring our gift to the altar, because we want to be reconciled to God. But those who want to be one with God must be one with their neighbors—all of them.

To be reconciled with our neighbors, we first have to recognize them. The command "Love your neighbor as yourself" actually means "Love your neighbor as a person like yourself." Recognize that no matter how different your neighbor may seem, he or she has equal dignity to you, and therefore demands your respect and love. Failure to protect the unborn is rooted in the failure to recognize them, which is the most fundamental kind of failure to love. The abortion controversy then becomes a matter of expressing beliefs rather than stopping bloodshed.

To be reconciled with our neighbors, furthermore, we have to respond appropriately to their needs. "If anyone is rich in worldly possessions and sees a brother in need but refuses to open his heart, how can the love of God abide in him?" (1 Jn 3:17) Is there anyone more in need than the child in the womb? Is there any need greater than to have one's life saved from a lethal threat?

To be reconciled to our neighbors, we must avoid false witness. To hold, in word or action, that the unborn are of less value than the rest of us, is to "bear false witness against your neighbor." If we are doing that, we are not ready to present our gift at the altar.

Communion means union, and union requires reconciliation. This applies to every citizen. How much more does it apply to those who, as public officials, have the opportunity to pass laws that either grant or remove protection from their most vulnerable neighbors?

Answering Pro-Abortion Politicians

I F you've ever written to a pro-abortion politician about the right to life, you've probably received a form letter that utilizes one of several worn-out arguments. Let's review how we answer them.

1. "I respect your views, but I have to represent all the people." Our response: That's what we're trying to say to you. If you neglect the unborn, you are not representing all the people. *Roe vs. Wade* excludes them from protection; we demand that they be included. A public servant should not ignore an entire segment of the public that is being destroyed.

2. "I'm personally opposed to abortion, but can't impose my views on others." Our response: This is not a matter of views, but of violence. The law is supposed to protect human life despite the views of those who would destroy it.

3. "The government should not be involved in such a personal decision as abortion." Our response: The government got "too involved" in abortion when it decided that it had the authority to deprive some human beings of their right to life. It is not up to government to grant this right. It's there already. Government exists to secure it. Moreover, when somebody's "choice" destroys somebody else's life, that choice is no longer merely a personal, private matter.

4. "Let's just agree to disagree." Our response: When victims are oppressed, we don't sit back and "agree to disagree" with the oppressor. Rather, we intervene to save the victim. Abortion is not about beliefs, but about

bloodshed. It's not about concepts; it's about protecting real people.

5. "Abortion is the law of the land." Our response: The "law of the land" can be changed, just as it was changed regarding slavery and segregation. Leadership means seeing the injustices that others miss, and inspiring people to utilize the methods the law permits to make necessary changes.

6. "I support women's rights and health." Our response: That is precisely why you should examine the evidence, which is more plentiful than ever, that abortion is destructive of women's health, and listen to the growing voices of those who have been harmed by abortion. That is also why you should examine how the abortion industry, through unregulated and dangerous clinics, continues to deceive and exploit women.

7. "Abortion is just one of many issues; I embrace a consistent ethic of life." Our response: The foundation of a house is only one of many parts of the house, but it is essential in order to build the other parts. That is why the Catholic bishops have repeatedly asserted that among the many interrelated issues within a consistent ethic, abortion deserves "urgent attention and priority" (Pastoral Plan, 2001).

8. "My office does not involve any decision-making about abortion." Our response: Your position on abortion says a lot about your character and worldview. If you cannot stand up for the smallest of children, how will you stand up for the rest of us?

Finally, always use the best response to all the arguments: I vote!

Part VIII

The Church

This Is My Body

DID you ever realize that the same four words that were used by the Lord Jesus to save the world are also used by some to promote abortion? "This is my body." The same simple words are spoken from opposite ends of the universe, with meanings that are directly contrary to each other.

When the Lord Jesus took bread, blessed it, broke it, and gave it to His disciples, saying, "This is My Body, which is given up for you," He was pointing to what would happen the next day, when He would give that same Body on the cross. He sacrifices Himself so that we may live. He gives up His Body so that He can destroy the power of sin and death. As a result, He welcomes us into His life, into His Kingdom. He makes us members of His Body!

On the other hand, abortion supporters say, "This is my body. So don't interfere with it! It's mine, so I can do what I want, even to the point of killing the life within it. All is secondary to my dominion over my body." In fact one abortion supporter has written, "I say their (pro-lifers') God is worth nothing compared to my body" (Michelle Goldberg, "Rant for Choice," in University of Buffalo student newspaper, 1995).

"This is my body." Same words, different results. Christ gives His body away so others might live; abortion supporters cling to their own bodies so others might die. In giving His Body, Christ teaches the meaning of love: I sacrifice myself for the good of the other person. Abortion teaches the opposite of love: I sacrifice the other person for the good of myself!

We never find happiness and fulfillment by pushing other people out of the way. We are fulfilled when we push ourselves out of the way. Pope John Paul II writes,

"He who had come 'not to be served but to serve and to give his life as a ransom for many' (Mk 10:45), attains on the cross the heights of love: 'No one can have greater love than to lay down his life for his friends' (Jn 15:13). And he died for us while we were yet sinners (cf. Rom 5:8).

"In this way Jesus proclaims that life finds its center, its meaning and its fulfillment when it is given up . . .

"We too are called to give our lives for our brothers and sisters, and thus to realize in the fullness of truth the meaning and destiny of our existence" (*Evangelium Vitae*, 51).

"This is my body." It is no accident that the same words are used for such different purposes. A spiritual conflict rages here. We win, in our own lives and in the world, by living these words in self-giving, life-giving love.

Should We Focus Just on Abortion?

THE Church is one body with many parts. The eye is not the hand, and those who focus on establishing soup kitchens are not the same as those who save babies at abortion mills. Each individual and group has a specific vocation and has a right (indeed, a duty) to focus on it.

So why belabor the obvious?

Because for some, it's not so obvious. Many of us who focus on abortion are told that we can't give a pro-life talk unless we mention all the life issues, or can't hold a pro-life event if it's going to focus just on abortion.

Excuse me, but why not?

Obviously, there are many life issues, and we are all called to see the connection between them. But seeing that connection, we are still free to focus. To have an event or preach a homily today on abortion means we also have the freedom to have an event or preach a homily next week that focuses on world peace.

Cardinal Joseph Bernardin is often invoked for his firm articulation of the consistent ethic of life. Yet he, too, made it clear that it is perfectly legitimate to focus on a particular issue. On one occasion he asked, "Does this mean that everyone must do everything? No! There are limits of time, energy and competency. There is a shape to every individual vocation. People must specialize, groups must focus their energies. The consistent ethic does not deny this. But it does say something to the Church: It calls us to a wider witness to life than we sometimes manifest in our separate activities" (Address at Seattle University, March 2, 1986).

When the US Bishops write about the consistent ethic of life, they say the following:

"Among important issues involving the dignity of human life with which the Church is concerned, abortion necessarily plays a central role. Abortion, the direct killing of an innocent human being, is always gravely immoral (*The Gospel of Life*, no. 57); its victims are the most vulnerable and defenseless members of the human family. It is imperative that those who are called to serve the least among us give urgent attention and priority to this issue of justice.

"This focus and the Church's commitment to a consistent ethic of life complement one another. A consistent ethic of life, which explains the Church's teaching at the level of moral principle—far from diminishing concern for abortion and euthanasia or equating all issues touching on the dignity of human life—recognizes instead the distinctive character of each issue while giving each its proper place within a coherent moral vision" (USCCB, *Pastoral Plan for Pro-life Activities*, 2001).

We are all called to be concerned about every life issue, and to say so. But it is the Church as a Body that is called to carry out the many works of justice, with each part of the body doing its appointed task rather than being made to feel it must do the task of everyone else.

The "Sacrament" of Abortion

THE *Sacrament of Abortion* is the title of a book written by Ginette Paris and published in 1992. In this short book, the author claims that abortion is a sacred act, a sacrifice to Artemis (known to the Romans as Diana).

Artemis is both a protector of wild animals and a hunter who kills them with deadly aim. How can these contradictory roles be found in the same female deity? The view proposed in Paris' book is that a mother properly cares for life only if she possesses full power over life and death. Death is sometimes preferable. The one who can provide death, in order that one may escape an unfriendly life, is really loving the one who is being killed.

Abortion, then, is seen as "an expression of maternal responsibility and not a failure of maternal love" (p. 8). "Artemis stands for the refusal to give life if the gift is not pure and untainted. . . . As Artemis might kill a wounded animal rather than allow it to limp along miserably, so a mother wishes to spare the child a painful destiny" (p. 55).

Artemis, of course, is the same goddess whose worshippers felt so threatened by Paul's proclamation of the Gospel in Ephesus, where a riot nearly broke out and a vast crowd shouted for two hours, "Great is Artemis of the Ephesians!" (Acts 19:34). The worshippers of Artemis today should likewise feel that their beliefs are threatened, because the proclamation of the Gospel of Christ is that He alone has authority over life and death. Neither the mother, nor the father, nor the state, nor the individual herself, can claim absolute dominion over life. "None of us lives for himself, and none of us dies for himself. If we live, we live for the Lord, and if we die, we die for the Lord. Therefore, whether we live or die, we are the Lord's" (Rom 14:7-8).

The fact that some defend abortion as a sacred act should alert us to the depth of the spiritual warfare that is going on. Abortion has never been merely or even primarily a political issue. It is a false religion. When pro-life Christians, for example, pray in front of an abortion mill, it is not simply a matter of pro-life people opposing false medicine. It is the true Church in conflict with a false Church. One former clinic security guard, after being converted, admitted why he was angry at pro-life sidewalk counselors: "You were coming to protest in front of our church. That clinic was where we conducted our worship."

May all believers, and their clergy, take renewed strength to speak out against abortion. Not only is doing so consistent with the proclamation of the Gospel; it *is* the proclamation of the Gospel.

My Days with Mother Teresa

I HAVE been thinking a lot these days about the time I spent with Mother Teresa in 1994, when she invited me to speak to sisters and priests in India about the work of Priests for Life. We had many discussions about the pro-life movement. When I told her about some of the legal persecution that pro-life people face, she looked at me and said, "Father, if we had laws like that here in India, I would have been thrown in jail many times!"

We discussed her February 3, 1994 speech at the National Prayer Breakfast, in which she told our government leaders that a country that allows a mother to kill her own child is not teaching its people how to love, but rather how to use violence to get what they want. I told her what an impact the speech made on the pro-life community. "What about the rest of the American people?", she asked me at once. She then gave me a homework assignment to spread the speech far and wide, which Priests for Life has been doing ever since.

Reflections on the life and work of Mother Teresa characteristically focus on her "love for the poor." She did love the poor. But her understanding of what poverty is was much more profound than that of most observers. To grasp it, we need to appreciate her message about the vocation of the human person. We were made to love and be loved, she would often remark. To give and receive love is the calling and greatness of human beings.

The fundamental poverty, then, is to fail to give and receive love. That is why a society which throws away its children by abortion is poorer than one which does not have many material resources. The society that permits abortion fails in its vocation to give love, to welcome the inconvenient person. To fail to love is poverty. To fail to love to the point where the other person is not even recognized as a person, and is legally destroyed, is poverty to the extreme.

Mother Teresa picked up the dying from the streets of Calcutta with the same love with which she pulled women away from abortion facilities. Love is indivisible. It means making room for the other person, whether that person is in the street or in the womb. It means feeding that person, not just with food for the body, but with the recognition, attention, and compassion that their personal dignity demands. This is why those who praise Mother Teresa's work "for the poor," but do not share her opposition to abortion, simply have failed to understand both.

We are called to give and receive love. As we rise above the culture of death, we will be free of the poverty that fails to welcome our brothers and sisters. We will, instead, sacrifice ourselves for them, and will discover the kind of riches which only grow greater the more we give them away.

Do I Believe in the Consistent Ethic of Life?

I AM sometimes asked if I "believe in" the consistent ethic of life.

Consistency is not something one simply "believes in"; it is something one is obliged to! In regard to the sanctity of life, consistency demands that we recognize and defend the dignity of the human person, whoever that person may be, wherever that person may be, and whatever threat to human dignity that person may face. Consistency in this regard is another way of saying that love is indivisible. To love "our neighbor" does not admit of exceptions. We are not free to exclude anyone from our love.

There seem to be two extremes in the way people respond to the consistent ethic of life.

One of those extremes sees the consistent ethic as a totally invalid and dangerous idea, which ruins the pro-life movement and is in fact a mark of those who are opposed to that movement.

Yet to take this position is itself dangerous, because the pro-life effort is not based on a principle of the sanctity of some human life, but on the sanctity of all human life, precisely because it is human!

The other extreme holds that all issues regarding human dignity are to be equated. As a result, those who talk about abortion are expected to talk about capital punishment, drug abuse, teen suicide, poverty, and, well, everything.

But that doesn't make too much sense either. To criticize someone for having a practical focus on abortion is comparable to criticizing Alcoholics Anonymous for having a practical focus on alcoholics!

In other words, everyone in the Church must adhere to a consistent ethic. But to translate that ethic into concrete action that responds to every issue involving human dignity is a task of the Church as a whole. The Church is one Body with many members, not all of which have the same function. To demand that every group in the Church address every issue also fails to take heed of something we all experience: the limitations of our time, resources, and energy!

In this context, the US bishops have spoken clearly: "Because victims of abortion are the most vulnerable and defenseless members of the human family, it is imperative that we, as Christians called to serve the least among us, give urgent attention and priority to this issue of justice . . . This focus and the Church's firm commitment to a consistent ethic of life complement each other. A consistent ethic, far from diminishing concern for abortion or equating all issues touching on the dignity of human life, recognizes the distinctive character of each issue while giving each its proper role within a coherent moral vision"(*Pastoral Plan for Pro-Life Activities, A Reaffirmation,* 1985, p. 3-4).

Criticism of groups that focus only on abortion is not a corollary of the consistent ethic. The sooner we get away from this misapplication of a very valid truth, the sooner we will enable the entire Church to see that the consistent ethic should indeed be embraced by all.

Compassionate and Truthful

THERE is no question I receive more often than, "Why don't our priests speak out more about abortion?"

Having directed the Priests for Life movement since 1993 and spoken every weekend in a different parish on the subject of abortion, I have had more opportunity than most to directly observe how people in the pews respond to the Church's pro-life message. I have also had more opportunity than most to speak to my brother priests about it.

One of the questions that many priests (and others who have a ministry in the Church) wrestle with is, "How can I be compassionate to my people and also forthright with them about the truth?"

The answer to this contains much of the answer to the question about preaching on abortion. The abortion issue involves pain—not only the pain experienced by those who have been directly responsible for one or more abortions, but also the pain of those who, watching abortion from a distance, know that they should do more to help stop it, but don't want to pay the price. That's a pain we all share.

So how do you balance truth and compassion?

You start by realizing that they are not things that have to be "balanced," as though they have some intrinsic opposition to each other. Rather, truth and compassion are aspects of the very same reality. God, who is One, is both Truth and Compassion. To represent God, to speak for Him, to somehow mediate Him, is to respond to the values of truth and compassion precisely as aspects of each other.

In other words, to have compassion for another human being is precisely to bear witness to the truth of who God is and who that person is. A failure in compassion is essentially false witness against our neighbor, because such a failure eclipses the infinite tenderness and mercy of the Lord.

At the same time, to withhold truth is to fail in compassion. It is to fail to meet a human need which is as real as food and shelter. Truth nourishes. Truth sets us free. A witness to truth truly ministers to his brothers and sisters.

We can err in the way we extend both truth and compassion. Truth is sometimes spoken harshly, and with a tunnel-vision that fails to understand where our audience really stands. Compassion is sometimes bestowed carelessly, failing to challenge the one we love to become all he or she is called to be, and failing to distinguish mercy from permission.

A key to more effective ministry regarding abortion, therefore, is more understanding about the relationship between truth and compassion, and a deeper examination of conscience regarding how we fail in bearing witness to both. The heart of the Christian, and in particular of the priest, must be the meeting place of a clear and prophetic stand against injustice, and a profound tenderness to those who have committed it.

Abortion in the General Intercessions

IN my seminary days, each student was responsible, on a rotating schedule, to prepare the general intercessions for the Eucharistic Liturgy of that day. This was an aspect of our liturgical training, of course, whereby we would apply the principles we had learned in the classroom.

The content and form of the General Intercessions (often referred to as "Prayers of the Faithful") do follow certain clear principles. They are general by nature. They are to reflect themes that are of concern to the entire Church. They are to embody the natural response of a Christian Community which, having been formed by the Word of God in the way they think and judge, now look at the world and what is going on in it. It makes sense, therefore, that these intercessions come at the point in the Mass just after the community has again heard God's Word proclaimed in the readings and the homily, and assented to in the Creed.

A frequent theme in these intercessions, and rightly so, is human suffering. The poor, the hungry, the sick, and those whose rights are trampled upon, are mentioned in these prayers. Indeed, *The Pastoral Constitution on the Church in the Modern World (Gaudium et Spes)* of the Second Vatican Council begins by affirming that the joys and hopes, as well as the sufferings, of all humanity, are likewise the joys, hopes, and sufferings of the Church. The General Intercessions are a particular moment of solidarity with our suffering brothers and sisters.

Nor do we tire of repeating their needs, because with each passing day, new people are involved in these forms of human suffering. We as priests do not refuse to take a sick call simply because we have taken a thousand of the same kind before. We as a community do not refuse to repeat, day after day and week after week, the needs of the poor, sick, and dying.

What, then, of our brothers and sisters in the womb? The law has called them non-persons, and abortion kills one of them every 23 seconds. Those killed today never died before, which makes abortion a new tragedy every day.

Nothing takes more human life.

Does it not make good Christian and liturgical sense to include this form of human suffering and vulnerability in our General Intercessions as frequently as we include any other? Is not a simple prayer for these children a powerful expression of our solidarity with those who cannot even pray for themselves?

The abortion tragedy has so many dimensions, furthermore, that a different angle can be addressed each time. We can pray for the children in danger, for the mothers and fathers in despair both before and after abortion, for lawmakers, for medical professionals, for people in the pro-life movement, for the pro-life ministries of the Church, and so forth.

In the light of such an immense tragedy, it really is the least we can do.

Using the Parish Bulletin to Save Lives

ABORTIONS can be stopped and lives can be saved long before laws are changed. The children scheduled to die tomorrow don't have time for legislators to pass laws to protect them. This is one of the ways in which the pro-life cause reveals itself to be much more than a "political" issue. It is an emergency to which the People of God need to respond here and now, to save the lives of the most defenseless among us. It is a concrete demand of charity.

There is a simple way we can activate our parishes to respond: Spread the phone numbers at which people can find alternatives to abortion.

And one of the most effective ways to spread them is not only to put them in the bulletin but to put them on the bulletin, in other words, right there on the front cover along with the other standard phone numbers that we always want to make known to our people. After all, the need for abortion alternatives is not seasonal or occasional, and, as a matter of life and death, certainly has priority importance over other numbers.

Studies and the experience of those who work with women in crisis pregnancy indicate that most do not know that there are alternatives to abortion, and most would choose an alternative if it were offered. I have seen women walk out of the waiting rooms of abortion facilities simply because they saw someone outside holding a sign offering alternatives.

The irony of the rhetoric "freedom of choice" is that women get abortions precisely because they feel they have no freedom and no choice. A simple phone number in the bulletin can change all that.

Now which numbers do we use? Certainly, local numbers through which people can contact resources in the diocese or community are always valuable.

As a national movement, Priests for Life also makes known national hotline numbers that can connect people to help in any part of the country. The criteria we use for which numbers we publicize are that they are 1) toll-free, 2) accessible 24 hours a day, 3) available from anywhere in the country, and 4) serviced by a live person at all times. You may wish to call the number yourself to find further information in order to determine which you want to publicize.

We therefore invite pastors to put one or more of these numbers somewhere on the cover of the bulletin as a permanent item.

One such number is the "Option Line," operated by large networks of pregnancy centers. The number is 1-800-395-HELP.

We invite parishioners to make this option known to their pastors.

Furthermore, these numbers can be posted in the vestibule, distributed in our high schools and colleges, put in parish mailings, and displayed in the local press or cable TV bulletin board. There is hardly a simpler thing that can be done for the pro-life cause. Let's not put it off until tomorrow!

The Covenant in My Blood

I BECAME a priest in 1988, and have often reflected on how many times I have celebrated the Sacrifice of the Mass. Above all those Masses, however, stands one which, beyond doubt, was the most moving and significant.

The room in which it was celebrated was very small, the altar quite simple, and the congregation numbered only a handful. I was in Baton Rouge, inside the American Holocaust Memorial. It is a building which used to be an abortion facility, but was acquired by pro-life people and converted into an historic and educational center which depicts the history and mission of the pro-life movement. It is well worth a visit.

The most stirring fact is that the room which is now the little chapel used to be one of the procedure rooms. In that very spot, the blood of innocent children once flowed. Now, the blood of another Innocent Person, Christ the Lord, was flowing. That room once saw the activity of those who "made a covenant with death" (see Wis 1:16); now we were engaged in the activity of the "new and everlasting covenant" (see Lk 22:20), sealed in the Blood of Christ. In that room was often repeated what happened to Abel when he was killed: the voice of your brother's blood is crying out to me from the ground (Gen 4:10); now in that same room Heaven heard the cry of the Blood which speaks more eloquently than that of Abel (see Heb 12:24).

There is cause for great alarm over the four thousand daily abortions in our land. Yet there is also cause for hope. The Blood of the new and everlasting Covenant is even more plentiful than the blood shed by abortion.

The Blood of Christ speaks more eloquently than that of Abel; it speaks more powerfully than that of the aborted babies. While the blood of the children cries out for vengeance, the Blood of Christ cries out for mercy: Father, forgive them, save them, reconcile them, heal them, sanctify them! We who proclaim the Gospel of Life proclaim the Gospel of Mercy. I know of someone who had 24 abortions. Even she can be forgiven, through the Blood of the New Covenant.

That Blood also binds us to one another and gives us responsibility for one another. To say that we are brothers and sisters is more than a metaphor. We are, in fact, closer to one another than we would be if we had the same parents. The Blood of Christ unites us. Nor are the unborn excluded from this, for "By his incarnation the Son of God has united himself in some fashion with every human being" (Vatican II, *Gaudium et Spes*, 22; see *Evangelium Vitae*, 2).

That Mass I celebrated in Baton Rouge will echo in my mind for all my life. Let it echo through the land as well, heralding the day when every abortion facility will be transformed from a place of death to a place where the Living God is honored and the New Covenant flourishes.

Bloodguilt

DEUTERONOMY 21:1-9 describes a ritual that God's people had to carry out whenever anyone was found slain and it was not known who did the killing. Scripture reads, "[Y]our elders and your judges shall come forth, and they shall measure the distance to the cities which are around him that is slain" (v. 2). Those from the nearest city then needed to sacrifice a heifer, and their elders were to pray these words: "Our hands did not shed this blood, neither did our eyes see it shed. Forgive, O Lord, thy people Israel, whom thou hast redeemed, and set not the guilt of innocent blood in the midst of thy people Israel; but let the guilt of blood be forgiven them" (v. 8).

What is happening here? Obviously, when innocent blood is shed, something happens in the land; something happens to the people in the land in their relationship to God, even if they are not the ones who shed the blood. As the account of the first murder makes clear, the innocent, though slain, still speak. "The voice of your brother's blood is crying to me from the ground" (Gen 4:10).

The people of God are bound up in an inescapable mutuality, a responsibility for one another that transcends their own choosing. We see again, in Isaiah 1:10-20, that God tells His people "Your hands are full of blood" (v. 15). They were not doing the killing, but because the killing was occurring in their midst, they had a responsibility to intervene. Hence the passage continues with the instructions, "Seek justice, correct oppression" (v. 17).

What of us? Our land is polluted with the innocent blood of tens of millions of aborted children. Is it enough in the sight of God that we ourselves have not done the killing? Scripture says this is not enough. We know where the killing is occurring, we know how, and we know who is doing it. Abortion is publicly advertised and advocated. Because it occurs in our midst, we are inescapably involved.

What, then, are we to do? We are to repent. We need to see abortion not just as somebody else's sin, but as our sin. Even if we have never participated in an abortion, we must ask forgiveness for it. It is easy to blame abortion on those who do it and support it. But we must also blame ourselves. This is a spiritual dynamic which has to undergird all of our other activities to end abortion. Usually, people think that the spiritual thing to do about abortion is to "pray." Truly, we must pray. But first and foremost we are called to repent, to take responsibility for the innocent blood that has been shed, and then to intervene to save the helpless.

Fortunately, the blood of another innocent victim also speaks. Jesus' blood "speaks more powerfully than even the blood of Abel" (Heb 12:24). Let us repent of abortion, wash ourselves in Jesus' blood, and get to work defending the innocent.

A Matter of the Heart

PRIESTS for Life thanks the United States bishops for their statement "A Matter of the Heart," issued in observance of the thirtieth anniversary of *Roe vs. Wade* (see www.priestsforlife.org/magisterium/bishops/matterof theheart.htm).

The statement is filled both with hope and determination, declaring that "*Roe vs. Wade* must be reversed," and also pointing out many signs of progress.

The word "heart" is used often in the statement. It speaks with special emphasis of the loving and hopeful hearts of the young. It speaks of the hearts of children broken by abortion. It speaks of the hearts of those tempted to abort, and broken by having aborted their child. The bishops point out that we must strive to know these hearts. We are no strangers to evil, temptation, and sin. We have all aborted God's will in our lives. We will know the hearts of the women and men ensnared by abortion to the extent that we strive with honesty and courage to know our own hearts.

The statement calls us to reach the hearts wounded by abortion, and give them hope. Abortion, indeed, is not only a sin against life, but a sin against hope. It says there is no future, no reason good enough to strive for life. To affirm life, on the other hand, is to say there is room for hope, and room to welcome the unwanted. Welcome opens the door to hope, and hope opens the door to life.

In calling for a ministry to the heart, the bishops also exercise it by their promise in this statement that the Church is ready to assist all who are pregnant and in need, and to accompany all who need repentance, healing and forgiveness.

The fact that the defense of life is "a matter of the heart" obviously does not exclude matters of the law, because this statement calls for a reversal in the law. The things of the heart and the things of the law affect each other in profound ways.

Yet evil, as our Lord told us, flows from what is in the heart. Nobody has to choose or tolerate abortion. No nation or public official should feel bound to uphold a "law of the land" that turns God's law upside down. The heart is free when it recognizes truth, and chooses what is good, despite the superficial attraction of evil. The heart is pure when it belongs to God, and thereby belongs to life.

The most fundamental sense in which the pro-life effort is "a matter of the heart" is that to end abortion, our hearts must be broken. This evil cannot simply be something we know about or debate. We have to allow it to grieve us, to bring us to tears, to bring us to our knees. "Blessed are those who mourn," for only when our hearts are broken can they open wide enough to receive the victory which has already been won, the victory of truth over lies, of hope over despair, of life over death.

Indeed, this is a matter of the heart.

Divine Mercy

POPE John Paul II gave a new gift to the pro-life movement.

You have likely seen the picture of Jesus standing with his hand pointed to his heart, from which red and pale rays emanate. The words "Jesus, I trust in you" are at the bottom. This image represents the devotion to Divine Mercy, based on revelations given to St. Faustina Kowalska (1905-1938). The image itself was revealed to her, as was the "Chaplet of Divine Mercy," in which we pray the following words:

"Eternal Father, I offer You the Body and Blood, Soul and Divinity of Your dearly beloved Son, Our Lord Jesus Christ, in atonement for our sins and those of the whole world. For the sake of His sorrowful Passion, have mercy on us and on the whole world."

Pope John Paul II fostered this devotion within the Church, and declared the Sunday after Easter to be Divine Mercy Sunday. Many of the faithful, especially in the pro-life movement, practice this devotion.

Indeed, the link between this devotion and abortion is established by St. Faustina herself and recorded in her "Diary." Fr. Seraphim Michalenko, MIC, who was a principal translator of St. Faustina's diary, and the postulator of her cause of canonization, writes the following:

"On at least three occasions, from 8:00-11:00 in the evening, she felt like her insides were being torn apart. She suffered so much that she thought she was going to die. The doctors couldn't figure out what was ailing her, and no medication was able to alleviate her sufferings. Later, she was given to understand that she was undergoing those pains for mothers who were aborting their children (Diary, 1276).

"On another occasion, she had a vision of an angel coming with thunderbolts to destroy one of the most beautiful cities of her country. And she felt powerless to do anything about it (Diary, 474). What antidote did the Lord give her? The Chaplet of Divine Mercy. [She explained] that the city was to be chastised for its sins, primarily the sin of abortion." ("Wombs of Mercy," *Marian Helpers Bulletin,* Summer 1995, p. 13).

Now the Pope has personally emphasized this connection once again, by signing a special Papal Blessing for those who pray the Chaplet for an end to abortion. The blessing, signed on the Feast of the Annunciation, March 25, 2003, is addressed to the Eucharistic Apostles of the Divine Mercy and to "all the faithful worldwide who join them in offering the Divine Mercy Chaplet . . . for mothers, that they not abort their offspring; for infants in danger of being put to death in the womb; for a change of heart of providers of abortions and of their collaborators; for human victims of stem cell research, genetic manipulation, cloning and euthanasia; and for all entrusted with the government of peoples, that they may promote the Culture of Life, so as to put an end to the culture of death."

God cannot fail to hear our prayer; let's not fail to pray it.

Matchup

THROUGH a special initiative of Priests for Life, the nation's 19,000+ Catholic parishes have now been "matched" to the nation's remaining 700+ freestanding abortion mills. Each parish is asked to pray and work for the conversion and closing of a specific killing center.

This project applies the spiritual power of the Church against the deadly power of the abortion industry. Obviously, we pray and work for an end to abortion throughout the nation. But abortion happens in specific, local abortion mills, and that's where it is most easily stopped.

This effort helps to focus and channel the energies of God's people in the pro-life battle. It provides simple ways that everyone in the parish—whether young or old, healthy or sick, mobile or homebound—can direct their prayers for an end to abortion. The success of the project, furthermore, is quite measurable.

The project is a form of "spiritual adoption," by which the entire parish, as a community, "adopts" the abortion mill, all the babies who are brought there, the mothers and fathers, the employees and volunteers, and all who help the mill to function. Look for the special prayer which has been composed for this purpose, and can be found, along with the listing of parishes and mills, at www.priestsforlife.org/mills. (If local circumstances make it seem advisable, the parish may change which abortion mill it focuses upon.)

The project aims not only for the closing of the mill, but for the conversion of all who help it to function, so that they never try to start another one.

The spiritual battle inherent in this project should not be underestimated. One former abortion mill security guard said to a pro-life leader that the mill was "a church—a place of worship." Ginette Paris, a pro-abortion author, actually wrote a book called *The Sacrament of Abortion,* calling this procedure a sacred sacrifice to the goddess Artemis. Some have bumper stickers that say, "Abortion is a woman's rite," and it is no secret that witchcraft is sometimes carried out inside abortion clinics. The lining up of the parishes with the mills is a face-off between the false church and the true Church; between the false god, who transforms suffering into violence, and the true God, who transforms violence into suffering; between the innocent blood of babies that cries out for vengeance, and the innocent Blood of Christ that cries out for mercy; between those who make a covenant with death, saying "This is my body, even if the baby dies," and those who renew the everlasting covenant of Life, saying, "This is My Body, given up for you, that you may live forever."

Our Lord told us that the gates of hell would not prevail against the Church. It is the Church that takes the initiative, storming the gates of sin with the power of grace, the gates of falsehood with the power of truth, and the gates of death with the power of life. And the gates will not stand.

Caught Sleeping

"I DON'T want the Church to be caught sleeping again . . ."

This is the heartfelt desire which the man who was a key player in bringing us legal abortion, Dr. Bernard Nathanson, has expressed to me regarding the bioethical challenges of the 21st century. Dr. Nathanson maintains that in the '60s, he and his colleagues at NARAL (at that time, the "National Association for the Repeal of Abortion Laws") literally "stole the issue" from the Church. In speaking to clergy, he says, "We would never have gotten away with what we did if you had been united, purposeful, and strong."

The new bioethical challenges have shaped the news and everyday discourse: embryonic stem cell research, genetic manipulation, and human cloning. Those who want to advance science-fiction agendas will still not get away with what they are doing if the Church is united, purposeful, and strong.

One of the many key insights which *Evangelium Vitae* provides about these issues is a play on words. The English word "matter" and the Latin word "mater" ("mother") express two ways of looking at creation, including human life. Pope John Paul II wrote, "[O]nce all reference to God has been removed, it is not surprising that the meaning of everything else becomes profoundly distorted. Nature itself, from being 'mater' (mother), is now reduced to being 'matter,' and is subjected to every kind of manipulation" (n. 22).

To put this another way, we can look at creation and consider how useful it is, or we can look at creation and reverently marvel at it. These two visions are not mutually exclusive. To marvel at the beauty of a tree doesn't mean we can't use it for lumber. But the danger lies in reducing our vision entirely to "matter." This is particularly dangerous when it comes to human life, because a person is not a thing, and is never to be treated as a thing. The drive to "use" embryos and their cells, and to "manipulate" the genetic code, necessarily puts the person in the category of a thing, despite any "good intentions."

The new bioethical challenges do not replace abortion as a central focus, because the assertion in *Roe vs. Wade* that "the word person . . . does not include the unborn" provides the foundation for the type of thinking behind these new challenges. As our bishops have pointed out, "Nations are not machines or equations. They are like ecosystems. A people's habits, beliefs, values and institutions intertwine like a root system. Poisoning one part will eventually poison it all . . . So it is with the legacy of *Roe vs. Wade*" (*Living the Gospel of Life*, 1998, n. 9).

The way out of this mess is not going to be easy. Sleeping is easy; vigilance has a price. Fundamentally, if the Church is not to be caught asleep again, we have to prioritize our activities, and devote more resources to both education and activism in the defense of life. This work cannot be a hobby; it will require us to give everything. But that should sound familiar to Christians.

Sexual Morality or Social Justice?

WHEN you think of the abortion issue, what category do you think of first: sexual morality or social justice?

Abortion, of course, has to do with both.

An abuse of human sexuality leads to a demand for abortion.

But abortion is a sin in a different category from abuses of human sexuality. It is a trampling of the most fundamental rights of another human being; it is a sin against justice.

The distinction appears in *The Gospel of Life*, where Pope John Paul II wrote,

"Certainly, from the moral point of view contraception and abortion are specifically different evils: the former contradicts the full truth of the sexual act as the proper expression of conjugal love, while the latter destroys the life of a human being; the former is opposed to the virtue of chastity in marriage, the latter is opposed to the virtue of justice and directly violates the divine commandment 'You shall not kill.'

"But despite their differences of nature and moral gravity, contraception and abortion are often closely connected, as fruits of the same tree" (EV#13).

Both the connection and the distinction need to be taught by the Church. The connection is rightfully receiving a lot of renewed attention in these days, both in Catholic and Protestant circles.

But an important strategic truth lies in acknowledging the distinction.

The general public normally views most sexual matters as purely matters of privacy. Witness the way so many people separated their evaluations of President Clinton's "private life" from his public "job performance."

Witness also how some supporters of abortion still use the slogan that "Government should stay out of the bedroom." Aside from the fact that abortions are not performed in bedrooms, but rather in (largely unregulated) public facilities advertised in the yellow pages, this slogan totally sidesteps the justice issue. If another person is being killed, even in the bedroom, the government has to impose sanctions, in order that vulnerable people may be protected.

Viewing abortion more from the social justice angle than from the sexual morality angle can also help priests to preach about it with more ease. Ask any priest what is easier to speak about: chastity or violence. Abortion is an act of violence.

Stressing this angle also helps to reinforce a consistent ethic of life. Why, after all, should there be a gap between the Church's efforts to speak up for the safety of non-combatants endangered by the bombs of war, and the safety of children endangered by the forceps of the abortionist? Why should it be any more difficult to see that we need to defend the victims of abortion than it is to see that we need to defend the victims of drugs, poverty, and AIDS?

Ultimately, to see abortion only in terms of sexual morality could feed the very problem the pro-life movement tries to counteract, namely, that the person in the womb has become the most ignored and forgotten among us. If that isn't about social justice, what is?

Death Penalty for the Innocent

FROM the beginning of my ministry, I have preached and taught consistently against the death penalty (see www.priestsforlife.org/deathpenalty.htm). I do not believe it should be used and have joined efforts to abolish it.

At the same time, there's a difference between capital punishment and abortion. Put simply, abortion can never be justified; capital punishment can sometimes be justified. Abortion is intrinsically evil, which means that no circumstances can ever make it right. Capital punishment, on the other hand, is evil when used in the wrong circumstances, but can sometimes be used in the right circumstances.

Capital punishment can never be carried out on an innocent person. That would defy its very definition. Abortion, on the other hand, is always carried out on an innocent person. Otherwise, that would defy its very definition.

In those rare circumstances where it has been justified, capital punishment was carried out precisely for the defense of life. Abortion, on the other hand, is carried out precisely for the destruction of life.

There is a substantial difference between a tiny child, growing in her natural environment, and a convicted criminal who poses a threat to the well-being of society. Yet more children are killed by abortion in America every five days than have ever been executed by capital punishment.

The Bible, and 2000 years of Catholic teaching, recognize the state's right and duty to protect its citizens, even by force.

Romans 13:1-5 reads,

"Let every person be subject to the governing authorities. For there is no authority except from God, and those that exist have been instituted by God. . . . For rulers are not a terror to good conduct, but to bad . . . If you do wrong, be afraid, for he does not bear the sword in vain; he is the servant of God to execute his wrath on the wrongdoer."

In his encyclical *The Gospel of Life*, Pope John Paul II made a clear distinction between a practical "no" to the death penalty and an absolute "no" to abortion. In regard to the state punishing wrongdoers, he writes, "the nature and extent of the punishment must be carefully evaluated and decided upon, and ought not go to the extreme of executing the offender except in cases of absolute necessity: in other words, when it would not be possible otherwise to defend society. Today however, as a result of steady improvements in the organization of the penal system, such cases are very rare, if not practically nonexistent" (56).

Then he goes on to say, in distinction, "If such great care must be taken to respect every life, even that of criminals and unjust aggressors, the commandment 'You shall not kill' has absolute value when it refers to the innocent person" (57).

Simply put, "You shall not kill" applies even to the criminal, but with exceptions. "You shall not kill" applies absolutely to the innocent (born and unborn), without exceptions.

Can one still be pro-life and support the death penalty in certain instances? The answer is yes.

Abortion vs. War

THIS essay requires extra effort to explain what it is not. It is not an evaluation of the war in Iraq or of any national leaders.

It is, however, an observation, on the level of moral principle, about the relationship between abortion, war, and being pro-life. And even there, I am limiting myself to a couple of very simple and specific points, and not an exhaustive analysis.

In his historic speech to the United Nations in 1965, Pope Paul VI cried out, "War never again, war never again!" The world must heed these words. They don't just mean, "Don't fight!" They mean that we have to make justice and human rights so secure that the need to fight disappears.

Many ask whether one can be a pro-life Catholic and support the war. The answer is yes, which is to say that Catholic and pro-life teaching do allow for circumstances in which war is justified, because sometimes war has to be waged precisely for the defense of life.

Even when war is justified, life is always lost in the process. But innocent life is never targeted, and that makes all the difference in the world. How many innocent lives, and how many children, have been deliberately targeted for destruction in the current war?

By comparison, every abortion deliberately targets and destroys a child; otherwise, it isn't even an abortion.

The purpose of war is not to kill the enemy, but rather to deprive the enemy of his ability to wage war and to destroy others' rights. There's a big difference between targeting military/communications equipment to disrupt the operations of the enemy, and just trying to kill as many people as you can.

No doubt, some will read this column and begin arguing with me that the war in Iraq is not justified. I am not arguing with them, but precisely pointing out that it is OK for them to come to that conclusion. It is also OK for someone else to come to the conclusion that the war is justified.

What is not OK is for someone to say, "You are not pro-life because you support the war." In fact, one may support the war precisely because he or she is pro-life and concludes that in this case, force is the only way to protect human life, human rights, and human freedom from the hands of those who would destroy it. Others may disagree with the conclusion, which is fine—but don't deny the other person's right to come to the conclusion.

And do not miss the profound difference with abortion. There is no room for interpretations or evaluations of whether abortion may be justified. It cannot be, because its very essence is the deliberate targeting and destruction of a child. In war, we do not target a single child, whereas every abortion targets a child. Catholic teaching allows more than one position on war, but it does not allow more than one position on abortion.

The Advocate

"IF anyone does sin, we have an Advocate with the Father, Jesus Christ the Righteous One" (1 Jn 2:1). The Lord Jesus is our Advocate. "He always lives to make intercession for us"(see Heb 7:25, Rom 8:34).

Yet the Lord Jesus promised on the night before He died, "I will ask the Father, and he will give you another Advocate to be with you always, the Spirit of truth"(Jn 14:16-17).

What is an advocate? An advocate pleads our cause, takes our side, conducts our defense. When we cannot pray, the Advocate prays within us (see Rom 8:26). When we cannot save ourselves, the Advocate saves us and lifts us up. When we dare not approach the God we have offended by sin, the Advocate gives us confidence by speaking words of pardon and mercy.

Our age needs an advocate more than ever, because of the culture of death, and what the Holy Father has called a "conspiracy against life," a "war of the powerful against the weak" (see *The Gospel of Life,* #12). We need an advocate that can assure us that no sin of which we repent is beyond forgiveness. We need an advocate, furthermore, to assure us that we can indeed embark upon a new culture of life.

But as people filled with the Holy Spirit, we do not only have an advocate; we become advocates. "As the Father has sent me, so I send you," the Lord said, as He breathed the Holy Spirit upon the apostles. "When the Advocate comes . . . he will testify on my behalf. And you also are my witnesses . . ."(Jn 15:26-27).

We also testify. We also advocate. If we cry out for mercy, can we indeed neglect the cries of others for mercy? If we know that we cannot save ourselves, can we be indifferent to others who cannot save themselves?

Sometimes in speaking of the babies in danger of abortion, we say that we all "were once in their position." Indeed we were. But in another way we still are. We still need to be saved. We cannot rescue ourselves from death. We still cannot speak for ourselves.

When the Holy Spirit came at Pentecost, He appeared as tongues of fire. He gave speech to the apostles, whose fear had wrapped them in silence. Despite great danger to themselves, they went forth and proclaimed Christ.

The Holy Spirit still comes, and we are still called to proclaim Christ. An essential aspect of that proclamation is "to proclaim good news to the poor . . . liberty to captives" (Is 61:1, Lk 4:18). The poor are not just those who have little. The poor are those who have no help but God. There is no group of people more helpless and more in need of an advocate than the children in the womb.

When we are filled with the Holy Spirit, the "father of the poor" *(Sequence of Pentecost)*, we advocate on behalf of the very poorest, threatened as they are by abortion. When we are filled with the Holy Spirit, who inspires our speech, we speak up for the pre-born. Then, indeed, we know the Advocate.

The Spirit of Truth

I HAVE always found one of the most fascinating aspects of theology to be the study of the gifts of the Holy Spirit: wisdom, understanding, knowledge, counsel, fortitude, piety, and fear of the Lord. Each has its own characteristics. Each has its own ways of lifting us up and transforming our lives.

The gift of knowledge helps us to see created things for what they really are. Together with a knowledge of God, we need a proper knowledge of creation, so that we may neither despise it nor worship it.

How do I understand reality? How do I proceed, then, to treat the created realities around me?

The Holy Spirit gives us a proper understanding of creation because He is the Spirit of Truth. "But when the Spirit of truth comes, he will guide you into all the truth" (Jn 16:13). He frees us from the lies we tell ourselves and each other. He frees us from the blindness which sin brings, a blindness that distorts our knowledge of God, creation, and our very selves.

Pope John Paul II has written of "how the value of life can today undergo a kind of 'eclipse' "(The Gospel of Life, #11), leading to such evils as abortion and euthanasia. We need the Spirit of Truth to lead us out of this eclipse.

The conviction that the child in the womb is not worthy of protection is not merely a statement about the child in the womb. It is a statement about all of us. It reflects a distorted answer to the fundamental question, "What is a human person?"

The Risen Christ proclaims in the Book of Revelation, "To anyone who is victorious, I will give the right to sit with me on my throne"(Rev 3:21). We will not only worship before the throne of God. We will sit with Him on the throne! That is the destiny of the human person! The Spirit bears witness to the greatness of our destiny by crying out "Abba, Father!" within us. The Spirit enables us to see the greatness of our calling, and the greatness of the same call given to every human being, including those yet in the womb.

This confronts the lie of abortion, which throws human beings in the garbage. Such an action in itself contradicts the Gospel. How can one who believes that the ultimate destiny of human beings is in the heights of heaven allow such human beings to be thrown away as trash?

Abortion does not only break the fifth commandment, Thou shalt not kill. It breaks the eighth commandment, Thou shalt not bear false witness against thy neighbor. To speak of or treat a human being as less than human is to bear false witness, to lie about his/her dignity.

We need You, O Spirit of Truth! Visit your people, and open their eyes and hearts once again to the greatness of human dignity and the sanctity of every life! Guide individuals and nations to recognize and defend the true meaning of human life. Amen.

The Spirit of Love

ST. Paul calls God the Father the one who "did not spare his own Son but gave him up for all of us" (Rom 8:32). He handed him over, that is, to the agony and disgrace of crucifixion between two thieves.

How can it be? How can the Father hand his Son over to that?

It is because the Father inspired in the Son such great love. That is how St. Thomas Aquinas answered the question. The Lord indeed had said, "No one has greater love than to lay down his life for his friends" (Jn 15:13).

The love which exists between the Father and the Son, and is poured out on us, is a Person, the Holy Spirit. He is Love.

"Love" is the most misused, abused, and confused word in the English language. We use it for a lot of good things, and for a few evil things as well. But in the Word of God we find its authentic meaning: "This is how we know what love is: he laid down his life for us" (1 Jn 3:16). The Holy Spirit is visible not only on Pentecost. In a very real sense, He becomes visible in the crucifixion, because the kind of love He inspires is the love that gives unto the point of death. Thus, the Letter to the Hebrews states, "Christ, . . . through the eternal Spirit offered himself without blemish to God" (Heb 9:14).

In the laws of the Old Testament, offerings were consumed by fire. In the eternal offering of Christ, the fire is the Holy Spirit.

But that same Holy Spirit is given to us. The second half of 1 John 3:16 states, "we in turn must be prepared to lay down our lives for our brethren." That's what love does. It gives itself away, and that is why it is the opposite of abortion. Love says, "I sacrifice myself for the good of the other person." Abortion says, "I sacrifice the other person for the good of myself." That turns the cross upside down and runs in the opposite direction of the Holy Spirit.

The love which gives itself away also unites. The Holy Spirit is the bond between the Father and the Son, and the one who unites the Church. "For in the one Spirit we were all baptized into one body . . . and we were all given the same Spirit to drink" (1 Cor 12:13). The Holy Spirit unites; abortion divides. You can't divide the human family more effectively than by introducing conflict between a mother and the child within her womb. Those who work with post-abortion counseling know the numerous other divisions abortion introduces within families and in the soul of those who have abortions.

I have read and written a lot of words about abortion over the years. But there are no words that can be said well enough, loud enough, or often enough to bring this tragedy to an end. That will happen only when, through the eternal Spirit, we too lay down our lives for our preborn brothers and sisters.

The Spirit of Confidence and Joy

SOME people like to describe themselves as "realists." They see aspects of reality that people who are overly optimistic miss.

It is important to be realists, but we need to carry realism to its full measure, and take account of all reality, including that which is unseen and supernatural. The problem with some forms of realism is that they stop at the realism of the problems of life, and miss the reality of grace. That's the formula for discouragement.

Doing pro-life work demands complete realism. And part of that complete picture is the reality, presence, and activity of the Holy Spirit, to whom the year 1998 was dedicated in the Church's preparation for the Jubilee of the Year 2000.

The Holy Spirit is the Spirit of confident joy. Joy is not the result of everything going our way. That kind of contentment is extremely fragile, because at any moment, any of the things going our way can begin going a different way.

Joy, on the other hand, is born of a deep inner awareness that our lives are in God's hands, that we are intent on pleasing Him, and that nothing short of our own rebellion can ever separate us from Him. Were we to lose all things, to possess God is to possess all. Being convinced of that, and actually possessing Him, brings joy.

Joy in our pro-life work is born of the fact that all we do is motivated by love: love for preborn children, their mothers and fathers, and love also for those who oppose what we stand for, whether they be in government, media, or the abortion industry itself.

Confident joy springs from the fact that this mission we have of restoring a culture of life is God's mission before it is ours. It is a mission we receive from the One who has all power to fulfill it and chooses to fulfill it through us.

How, then, can we not be confident? It is the Holy Spirit who fills us! It is the same Spirit who breathed over the waters and brought forth life out of chaos and darkness. It is the same Spirit who has spoken through the prophets, the same Spirit who descended upon the womb of Mary, the same Spirit who anointed the Lord Jesus and raised Him from the dead! The same Holy Spirit who sent the apostles sends us, and He has lost none of His strength. This, indeed, is the same Spirit who descends on bread and wine to transform them into the Son of God, and who will descend on our own tombs to raise us from the dead!

I am sometimes asked whether I become depressed dealing with abortion all the time. I would, I reply, were it not for one fact: I am proclaiming the victory of life. Let us do so together, with all the joy and confidence that the Holy Spirit brings.

Ending Abortion, Not Just Fighting It

A FRIEND recently asked me why I speak so often about "ending" abortion as opposed to just "fighting" it. There are a few reasons.

First, we have no other choice. Our nation, and civilized society as such, cannot continue to exist for very long on a basis that allows the destruction of little babies. Permission of the choice to kill the innocent does not provide a stable foundation for a society, because it removes the basis by which not only the unborn but everyone else in that society enjoys the protection of their lives. If a government can decide that one group of human beings are not persons, it can decide the same for other groups as well. If freedom of belief justifies violence against a baby, it justifies violence against anyone. We therefore have to bring abortion to an end. The abortion battle is not a matter of "Pro-life wins or pro-choice wins," but rather of "Pro-life wins or nobody wins."

Second, the Gospel requires it. The demands of the Gospel are high. The responsibilities both of justice and of charity rest not only upon individuals but upon entire societies. We are not permitted to exclude anyone from our love. To fail to secure the basic rights of the unborn is to fail to love them. We cannot "settle" for less.

Third, it is possible. I speak about "ending" abortion because it is a goal we can achieve. Yes, abortion has always been around. So have other sins. But we live today in a culture of abortion, which enshrines it in law, celebrates it as a right, and resorts to it with an alarming frequency that surpasses every other act of violence. That is something that can be turned around. A culture can be created in which abortion is not only illegal, but unthinkable. We can bring society to the point where, both in theory and practice, it regards abortion as it regards slavery today.

We can end abortion because the Lord has promised that "the gates of the netherworld will not prevail against [the Church]" (Mt 16:18). When we hear these words, we usually think, "The Church will survive all the attacks launched against her," and certainly that is true. But in a battle, a gate does not run out into the battlefield to attack the enemy. Rather, the gate stands still and defends the city against the enemy attacking it! When the Lord says the gates of hell will not prevail against the Church, He means that the Church is taking the initiative and storming the gates! Those gates of hell cannot withstand the power of heaven; gates of sin melt in the presence of saving grace; gates of death fall in the presence of eternal life; gates of falsehood collapse in the presence of living truth; gates of violence fall in the presence of divine love.

Abortion, indeed, will flee in the presence of the People of Life!

About the Author

FR. FRANK A. PAVONE is one of the most prominent pro-life leaders in the nation. He was born in Port Chester, New York and has been active in the pro-life movement since 1976. Cardinal John O'Connor ordained him to the priesthood in 1988. Fr. Pavone did parish work and taught in seminaries. In 1993, with the permission of Cardinal O'Connor, he became National Director of Priests for Life. In this full time position, he has traveled to all of the fifty states and to five continents, preaching and teaching against abortion and helping other priests to do the same.

He conducts seminars on pro-life strategy and is regularly invited to speak at national and international pro-life gatherings. Fr. Pavone appears often on national programs such as *Larry King Live, Good Morning America, The O'Reilly Factor,* and other shows on all the major networks. He is quoted in papers such as the *New York Times* and the *Los Angeles Times.* He is seen daily on EWTN and heard on Vatican Radio. His publications are distributed worldwide. He was with Terri Schiavo in her final moments and was an outspoken advocate for her life.

Under Fr. Frank's leadership, the Priests for Life staff has grown to 50 full-time employees.

Blessed Mother Teresa asked Fr. Pavone to address the clergy of India on the life issues. He has addressed the pro-life caucus of the United States House of Representatives, and was asked by the Vatican to help co-ordinate pro-life activities throughout the world as an official of the Pontifical Council for the Family. Norma McCorvey, the "Jane Roe" of the Supreme Court's abortion decision *Roe vs. Wade,* called Fr. Pavone "the catalyst that brought me into the Catholic Church."

In 1999, Fr. Pavone was named among the Top 100 Catholics of the Century. He serves on Dr. James Dobson's Focus on the Family Institute. The National Right to Life Committee awarded him their highest honor, the Proudly Pro-life Award. The Franciscan University of Steubenville bestowed on him an honorary doctorate, in recognition of his pro-life work. Fr. Pavone currently serves as President of the National Pro-life Religious Council, a coalition of groups from many different denominations working to end abortion. He is also Pastoral Director and Chairman of the Board of Rachel's Vineyard, an international retreat program for post-abortion healing. In 2006, Fr. Frank became the first Moderator General of the Missionaries of the Gospel of Life (M.E.V.), a community of priests permanently dedicated to full-time pro-life work.

Priests for Life

THE mission of Priests for Life is to encourage and equip God's people to respond to the tragedies of abortion and euthanasia. It is an Association of the Faithful recognized under the Canon Law of the Catholic Church. Priests, deacons, and lay persons may join as members simply by contacting the main office. Priests for Life is also a 501(c)3 tax-exempt organization.

This material may be reproduced or quoted, with proper credit, to spread the pro-life message.

To receive free pro-life commentary from Fr. Frank, you can request it at subscribe@priestsforlife.org.

You can contact Priests for Life at: PO Box 141172, Staten Island, NY 10314, Tel. 718-980-4400, Fax 718-980-6515, Email: mail@priestsforlife.org; Web site: www.priestsforlife.org

St. Joseph NEW AMERICAN BIBLES

FAMILY EDITION

Truly the most elegant of all. Here is an exceptionally fine Catholic Bible for the entire family to enjoy for many years. Durable sewn binding. Largest print of any Family Bible. Words of Christ printed in red. Over 100 Full-Color illustrations. Distinctive Family Record Section. GIFT BOXED. 1752 pages. 8½ x 11.

No. 612/97 ISBN 978-0-88842-612-9   **$55.95**

DELUXE GIFT EDITIONS
Full Size

Large, easy-to-read type, with 90 full-color illustrations, presentation page, colorful 8-page Family Record, Rosary & Stations in full color, over 70 photographs, Bible Dictionary, self-explaining maps, ribbon marker. Sewn binding. GIFT BOXED. 1696 pages. 6½ x 9¼.   **$45.00 each**

No. 611/13B Black Bonded Leather
ISBN 978-0-89942-971-7

No. 611/13W White Bonded Leather
ISBN 978-0-89942-972-4

No. 611/13BN Brown Bonded Leather
ISBN 978-0-89942-973-1

No. 611/13BG Burgundy Bonded Leather
ISBN 978-0-89942-970-0

DELUXE GIFT EDITIONS
Medium Size

Large, easy-to-read type, over 30 full-color illustrations, presentation page, colorful 8-page Family Record, Rosary & Stations in full color, Bible Dictionary, self-explaining maps, ribbon marker. Sewn binding. GIFT BOXED. 1632 pages. 5½ x 8⅛.   **$36.00 each**

No. 609/13BN Brown Bonded Leather ISBN 978-0-89942-959-5

No. 609/13W White Bonded Leather
ISBN 978-0-89942-958-8

No. 609/13R Red Bonded Leather
ISBN 978-0-89942-957-1

LITURGY OF THE HOURS—4-Volume Sets

This is the official English edition of the Divine Office that contains the translation approved by the International Committee on English in the Liturgy.

No. 409/10
Imitation Leather Binding
ISBN 978-0-89942-409-5
$149.00

Large Type Edition - **No. 709/13**
Color Leather Binding
ISBN 978-0-89942-710-2   **$198.00**

No. 409/13
Black Leather Binding
ISBN 978-0-89942-411-8
$175.00

www.catholicbookpublishing.com